CW01508436

The County Down Ti 1934 to 19

Donaghadee and Bangor

Paul Robinson

Published by Paul Robinson - robinsonbooks.co.uk

Copyright Paul Robinson 2024 except where indicated.

Printed by ESP Colour, Swindon, England

MICHAEL SEDGWICK
MEMORIAL TRUST

The County Down Trophy Races 1934 to 1936 is published with the financial assistance of the Michael Sedgwick Memorial Trust. The M.S.M.T. was founded in memory of the motoring historian and author Michael C. Sedgwick (1926-1983) to encourage the publication of new motoring research and the recording of Road Transport History. Support by the Trust does not imply any involvement in the editorial process, which remains the responsibility of the editor and publisher. The Trust is a Registered Charity, No 290841, and a full list of the Trustees and an overview of the functions of the M.S.M.T. can be found on www.michaelsedgwicktrust.co.uk.

Front cover: H C McFerran, Bangor West railway bridge. Photo Bugatti Trust.

A note on photographs

The photographs in this book are of varying quality from excellent to really quite poor. Many are copies of prints, others were produced from glass plate negatives and quite a few are scanned images. Regardless of quality all help explain some aspect of the races or identify a particular car or driver.

Photo editing was limited to cropping images or trying to improve their clarity. Nothing has been added or removed from within any of the photographs using AI or other software.

Tracking down photographs of 1930s Northern Ireland motor races is very difficult. National papers and motor sport magazines did not normally send photographers to races in Northern Ireland, relying on regional newspapers and/or freelance photographers.

Some of the best photographs of these races were taken by photographers working for the Belfast newspapers, for example The Northern Whig and The Belfast News-Letter. The photograph libraries of both these newspapers were destroyed in the 1970s as a result of IRA car bombs.

I am very grateful to everyone who searched through family albums and collections for the photographs used in this book. All photographs have been correctly attributed to the best of my knowledge. Any mistakes are mine.

Road Races in County Down 1928 to 1936

1. Ulster Tourist Trophy Races at Ards 1928 to 1936
2. County Down Trophy Race Donaghadee 1934
3. International County Down Trophy Race Bangor 1935 &
   1936

Contents

Acknowledgements

This book would not have been possible without the help and encouragement of the people listed below and many others.

Clare Ablett, Ulster Folk and Transport Museum

Peter Allen, Ulster Automobile Club

Terence Bradley, Ulster Vintage Car Club

Patrick Collins, National Motor Museum

Dave Cox, Pre 1940 Triumph Owners Club

Godfrey Evans, British Motorsport Marshals Club

Ralph Ewing, Ulster Automobile Club

Paul Gibbons and colleagues, Bugatti Trust

Dermot Johnson, Ulster Vintage Car Club

Simon Johnston, Ulster Vintage Car Club

John S Moore, MG Car Club

Robin McCullough and colleagues, Royal Irish Automobile Club

Jonathan Magee, North Down Museum

Briege Stitt, Downpatrick Library

Simon Thomas, Ulster Vintage Car Club

David Wylie, Ulster Vintage Car Club

Abbreviations

CC	Cubic centimetres
D	Pre-decimal pence (from the Latin denarii)
DNS	Did not start
GPO	General Post Office
H'cap	Handicap (usually in seconds)
HP	Horse Power
IAC	Irish Automobile Club
IMRC	Irish Motor Racing Club
Min	Minute or Minutes
N'Ards	Newtownards
PRONI	Public Records Office Northern Ireland
RAC	Royal Automobile Club
RIAC	Royal Irish Automobile Club
S	Shilling (pre decimal currency)
SC	Supercharged
Secs	Seconds
UAC	Ulster Automobile Club
UASC	Ulster Automobile Sports Club

Introduction

The most famous motor road races held in Northern Ireland are the Royal Automobile Club (RAC) Tourist Trophy races at Ards (1928 to 1936) and Dundrod (1950 to 1955).

Persuading the RAC to hold the first Tourist Trophy (TT) in Northern Ireland in 1928 was the culmination of six years of work by Harry Ferguson and others starting with the Northern Ireland parliament passing legislation in 1922 allowing public roads to be closed for motor racing.

The Ulster TT races at Ards attracted some of the best racing drivers in the world along with enormous crowds of spectators. They were also very expensive to hold and, despite generous government support, the organisers often struggled to cover the cost.

The TT races were not the only competitive motor events held in Northern Ireland. The Ulster Automobile Club (UAC), formed in 1925, had a full calendar of events including hill climbs at Ballybannon and Craigantlet, speed trials and races on Magilligan Strand and, starting in 1931, the Ulster Motor Rally (which later evolved into the Circuit of Ireland Rally).

In 1934 the UAC decided to introduce a road race open to all types of car, unlike the TT races which were in theory for standard production touring cars. It would provide a local event where Northern Ireland drivers (and others) could get experience of road racing.

The first County Down Trophy Race was held on a 3.75 mile triangular course at the small seaside town of Donaghadee. The 1935 and 1936 races gained international status and were held on a 5.94 mile course in nearby Bangor.

The County Down Trophy Races were smaller than the TT races but rapidly grew in importance attracting 50,000 plus spectators. They evolved into the International Ulster Trophy races at Ballyclare and Dundrod which attracted some of the biggest names in international motor racing including at least two world champions.

Please note the newspaper articles reflect the language and the times when they were written. For example the south of Ireland was officially called the Irish Free State in the 1930s and only later did the name change to the Republic of Ireland.

I have tried to include the relevant information on each race, entrant and driver, supported by photographs where possible, but there are gaps. For example I have not been able to identify the race number for every car and there are some drivers and cars I have very little information on.

This is the remarkable story of when grand prix and sports cars raced on small country roads at Donaghadee and along the streets in Bangor.

I hope you enjoy the book.

Paul Robinson

Background

In 1922 the Northern Ireland motorcycle and motor car communities pressurised the newly formed Northern Ireland parliament to pass legislation to allow motor races on public roads. Their ambition was to hold (separate) motorcycle and motor car grand prix races on a course north of Belfast in June that year.

The June target was missed but in October the first Ulster Motorcycle Grand Prix was held on the Clady course, between Belfast and Antrim. It was a motorcycle only affair; the motor trade had not recovered from the impact of the first world war and was badly affected by the Irish civil war.

While motorcycle racing grew from strength to strength the first motorsport event for cars in Northern Ireland did not take place until July 1924. Organised by the Ulster Division of the Motor Trade Association it was a hill climb at Red Brae, on the outskirts of Carrickfergus in County Antrim. It was to be the precursor for an Ulster Motor Grand Prix in October, two weeks after the Ulster Motorcycle Grand Prix and using the same Clady course.

In a cruel turn of fate one of the organisers of the event, Stanley Pyper, was killed during unofficial practising on the course a few days before it was due to be held. This lead to the race being postponed and eventually cancelled altogether.

The Motor Trade Association was devastated by the death of one their own members and had to bear the not inconsiderable cost of the cancelled event. The Association must also have been keenly aware of the unfavourable comparison between made between their attempt to run a motor grand prix and the very successful Ulster Motorcycle Grand Prix which had been running annually since 1922.

Motorcycle racing was organised by motorcycle clubs, for example the Motorcycle Union of Ireland Ulster Centre, but at that time there was no car club equivalent in Northern Ireland.

The Ulster Automobile Sports Club (UASC) was established on 11 September 1925 at a meeting in Chichester Street, Belfast. The first event it organised was a hill climb at Ballybannon, Castlewellan, a few weeks later on 3 October. The event was a great success and in 1926 was followed by racing and speed trials on Magilligan Strand.

In 1927 UASC members set out to persuade the Royal Automobile Club (RAC) to hold the British Grand Prix in Ulster rather than at Brooklands. All the other Grand Prix races in Europe were held on road courses it was argued. It proved impossible to prise the British Grand Prix from Brooklands grasp but the RAC, swayed no doubt by Harry Ferguson's promise of government support, agreed to hold the Tourist Trophy races in Northern Ireland.

The first Tourist Trophy (TT) race was in 1905 on the Isle of Man and the races continued to be held there until 1922. It was an enormous coup for Northern Ireland to get the TT race in 1928 and no effort was spared to make the race on the Ards course a success.

The following year the UASC decided, in addition to Ballybannon Hill Climb in June, to organise a hill climb at Craigantlet in August, the Saturday before the TT race. The hope was this would tempt competitors and tourists to come over to Northern Ireland a week early and thereby boost the local tourist trade.

In 1930 the British Automobile Racing Club (BARC) was approached to see if they would be interested in holding two different races on the road circuit used for the TT races. The first for racing cars and the second a Le Mans type 24 hour race. BARC declined, no doubt worried what impact this might have on their own income from race meetings.

In 1931 the UASC, in a further attempt to boost tourism, came up with a 500 mile Ulster Motor Rally which was also held in August, after Craigantlet Hill Climb and before the TT races. The start was in Belfast and the finish, a Concours D'elegance and prize giving, were in Bangor, County Down. First prize for the rally was £100 cash, a very generous amount during the great depression, donated by the residents of Bangor. The Rally along with Craigantlet Hill Climb and the TT races were promoted as Ulster Motor Week.

The combination of Craigantlet Hill Climb, the Ulster Motor Rally and the TT races in August proved very successful in attracting both competitors and spectators. The Ulster Motor Rally would eventually become the Circuit of Ireland International Rally and Craigantlet Hill Climb would become a round of the British Hill Climb Championship when it started in 1947. It still takes place on the same course each year.

The Ulster Automobile Club (Sports was dropped from the name in 1932) held its last hill climb at Ballybannon in 1933. Despite the historic significance of the venue (it is the oldest international hill climb venue in Ireland) the club was well aware that interest in it was declining. The performance of even ordinary production cars, in terms of speed, handling and braking, had great improved since the club held its first event there in 1925 and the long straight hill was not the challenge it had been.

Despite the success of Ulster Motor Week the 1933 TT Race had only 25 starters, the lowest number since it came to Northern Ireland. An article on the future of the TT in Irish Auto Sport on 31 January 1934 stated *"There was a feeling that after the 1933 event that it would possibly the last of its type."* It went on to say that the Royal Automobile Club (RAC) *"anxious to ascertain the views of those interested as to the sort of race for which there was the most general demand, circularised former entrants and manufacturers early this year asking for their opinions."*

The Northern Ireland motorsport community was worried that the RAC would cancel the TT races or move them to another location (possibly back to the Isle of Man).

They were also aware of the Irish Motor Racing Club plans for a new round the houses race in Bray, County Wicklow, 14 miles (approx) from Dublin City centre. The race was called Cuairt Bhré (Visit Bray in English).

The UAC concluded that the best way forward was to organise their own road race, but not on the Ards TT course. Something smaller, easier to organise, more affordable and less daunting than the TT. First they would have to find the roads for this new race and a sympathetic local council prepared to work with the club to make it happen.

The Importance of railways

"When the first world war ended in 1918 the dominant form of transport in Ireland and elsewhere, was the railway. For three-quarters of a century practically all the long distance passenger and freight traffic had been carried by rail and roads were used by those who were travelling or moving goods only short distances or could not afford train fares." (Road Versus Rail, PRONI)

Motor sport (two wheels and four) in Northern Ireland grew rapidly after the legislation to allow public roads to be closed for road racing was introduced by the Northern Ireland Parliament in June 1922.

 The organisers of motor racing events needed thousands of spectators for the events to be viable but, as recently as 1921, there were only 3,282 private cars[1] in Northern Ireland. Up until 1939 having one or more railway stations close to a course was essential to attract spectators traveling more than a few miles.

The RAC Tourist Trophy Races between 1928 and 1936 at Ards attracted up to 250,000 spectators annually (some reports state twice that number) and many travelled from all over Ireland via railway to Belfast or from different parts of Britain via rail and ferry. The start and finish of the TT was in Dundonald, on the edge of east Belfast and the course passed through the towns of Newtownards and Comber returning to Dundonald.

The London Midland and Scottish (LMS) Northern Counties Committee Railway, Great Northern Railway (GNR) and Belfast & County Down Railway (B&CDR) networks converged at Belfast and from there spectators could travel on to B&CDR

---

[1] Road Versus Rail, page 31

stations at Dundonald, Newtownards and Comber. Alternatively they could use the Belfast Corporation trams.

Donaghadee was one of the most important ports in Northern Ireland in the 17th, 18th and 19th centuries due to its proximity to Scotland had its own B&CDR station beside the docks. By 1934 the amount of commercial traffic on the railway was greatly reduced but the town attracted day trippers and holiday makers. The start/finish of the County Down Trophy Race was on the other side of town from the railway station but still only a short walk away.

The International County Down Races in Bangor (1935 and 1936) had the best railway connection of all. The start/finish line and pits were right in front of Bangor railway station and the grandstand was on the opposite side of the road.

Two Alfa Romeo cars in front of Bangor Railway Station, County Down Trophy Race 1935. Photo Dermot Johnson Snr.

Donaghadee 1934

Since the UAC was established in 1925 it had a reasonably good working relationship with Down County Council who (with the exception of 1926) had issued road closing permits for their hill climbs at Ballybannon, Croft (Holywood), Craigantlet and to the RAC for the TT races.

The decision to hold the new race in County Down, on the basis that it was replacing Ballybannon, would mean no increase in the number of road closing permits - one in, one out as it were.

The UAC had also built an excellent relationship with Bangor Town Council. From when it started in 1931 the Ulster Motor Rally finished in Bangor plus a Concours D'Elegance competition and the rally prize giving were also held there. In January 1934 the Mayor of Bangor was elected as one of the two UAC Vice-Presidents.

Donaghadee was also familiar to the UAC - for quite a few years the club night trial events finished there.

Articles in the local press and the UAC magazines point to the course at Donaghadee being chosen, in part, because sections of only three roads needed to be closed and alternate roads existed for traffic going in and out of Donaghadee from Bangor or Newtownards. Plus there was the added benefit of a Belfast & County Down Railway station which would greatly help spectators reach the course.

The UAC approached Down County Council at the beginning of 1934 seeking permission to hold the race on a 3.75 mile triangular course on the outskirts of Donaghadee.

The Council's Finance, Law and Parliamentary Committee submitted a report on the UAC proposal to the Down County Council half-yearly meeting in Downpatrick on 15 February.

The Newtownards Chronicle newspaper (24 February 1934) report on the meeting states:

"The Ulster Automobile Club had asked for permission to hold a new 100 mile road race near Donaghadee for motor cars in substitution for the Ballybannon hill climbing contest which has been held for some years.

The County Surveyor reported that the proposed course was formed by the Donaghadee-Bangor (inland) Road, Route B21, 1 1/2 miles; Donaghadee to Newtownards Road, Route A48, 1 1/2 miles; No 133 Ballyminetragh Road, 3/4 of a mile - total distance 3 3/4 miles.

The portion of the Ballyminetragh road had been steam rolled a number of years ago, and was in reasonably good order for a third class road. The carriageway varied from 12 to 14 feet wide with a grass margin on each side. As regards the surface, the County Surveyor feared that racing cars would injure it, particularly if the weather was very dry."

The committee recommended that permission be granted for the closing of the roads for an agreed number of hours on the day of the race and for practice on the previous day subject to the following conditions:

- The portion of the Ballyminetragh Road[2] used for the race being tarred (estimated cost £65);
- The Ulster Automobile Club informing the Committee how much it would contribute to this cost and
- The Club meeting the cost of advertising, erection of barricades, etc as in other races.

In a subsequent official statement the UAC confirmed that negotiations regarding costs were ongoing and *"the entire*

---

[2] This road has been renamed and is now the Kylestones Road.

circuit will have to be examined by a representative of the RAC and the agreement of the Kent and Sussex Light Car Club, who will be holding speed trials at Lewes on 16 June, also has to be obtained for the Ulster Club to run an event on the same day."

"In the preliminary arrangements, the club has received most willing and valuable assistance from Mr R J Dickson and Mr J G Wilkin, secretary and surveyor respectively of the Down County Council, and Mr R J McWhinney, Town Clerk of Donaghadee."

The three corners on the course were:

1. Hairpin
2. McCoubrey's
3. Angus

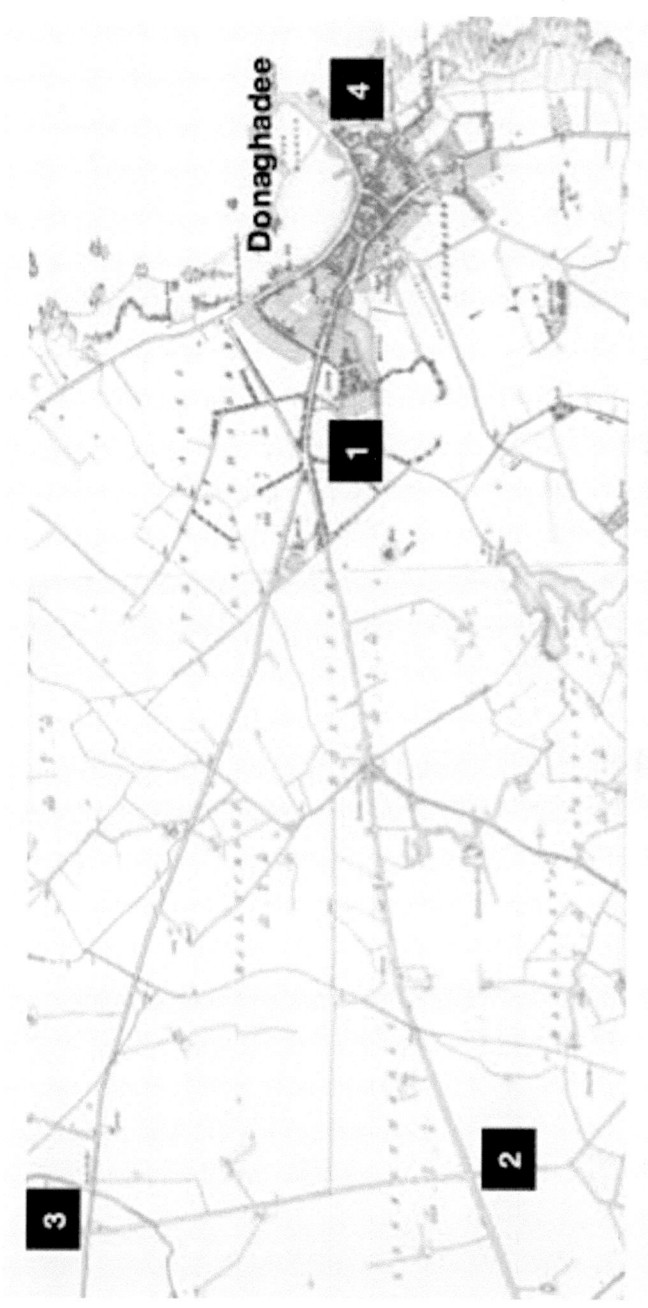

Donaghadee. Source OS County Series 1838-1862
1.Hairpin and start. 2. McCoubrey's corner. 3. Angus corner. 4. Railway station

The County Down Trophy Race

The Belfast Telegraph (10 March 1934) and North Down Herald (17 March 1934) ran articles announcing the decision at a meeting of the Ulster Automobile Club to call the 100 mile road race the *"County Down Trophy"*, the North Down Herald adding that this was *"in recognition of the interest and support which the sport of motor racing has received from the local authorities and inhabitants of County Down."*

Both newspapers reported that the committee meeting was chaired by the Right Honourable J Milne Barbour, DL MP, president of the UAC, and that RAC representative Captain A W Phillips MC would visit Belfast on 20 March to inspect the proposed course.

The list of awards was also published in each paper:

To the entrant of the first car - the County Down Trophy and £50.

To the entrant of the second car - a replica of the trophy and £25.

To the entrant of the third car - a replica of the trophy and £10.

To the entrant of the fourth car - a replica of the trophy and £5.

In addition there would be a team prize of fifteen guineas.

SUGGESTIONS FOR FORTHCOMING DONAGHADEE RACE
100 Miles Too Short

The above headline appeared in the Northern Whig newspaper on 17 March 1934 comparing the organisation of the Cuairt Bhré (Bray) road race with those of the UAC for the County Down Trophy.

Using the pen name "SUPERCHARGER" the writer praised the Irish Motor Racing Club (IMRC) stating the Bray event was being organised on a *"splendid scale" and the arrangements included "a dinner after the race for drivers and officials, followed by a dance,"* adding that the IMRC *"does not believe in running the race and then sending everybody home afterwards."*

By comparison *"the policy of the Ulster Automobile Club as far as racing is concerned seems to lack the "punch" of the Irish Motor Racing Club."* In addition to the UAC needing to get *"its publicity skates"* on the writer suggested that the event should be at least 150 miles or 40 laps of the circuit. This was on the grounds that the need for most competitors to re-fuel *"would add to the interest from the spectators point of view"* and the residents of Donaghadee were unlikely to object to the roads being closed for an extra hour (given the alternative routes into the town available).

Pointing to the enthusiasm the town of Bray had for their race the writer asked *"can the Ulster Club put the Donaghadee district on the spot?"*

Captain Phillips visits

Most of the local papers reported on the visit on the 20 March. The Northern Whig, returning to its normal position of lavishly praising Ulster motor racing, referred to the "prospects of a more-brilliant-than-ever Ulster motor racing season (the article was not written by SUPERCHARGER).

*"Captain A W Phillips, MC, from Royal Automobile Club headquarters, London, visited Belfast to discuss arrangements for the 1934 TT and to inspect the County Down Trophy Race course near Donaghadee, for which the Ulster Automobile Club are seeking a permit to run the event in July,"**

Captain Phillips, the RAC Press Secretary, inspected the course on the morning of the 20 March accompanied by William Noble (UAC chairman), Captain W J Thompson (UAC Secretary), Fred Rodgers (Chairman of the Ulster Committee for the TT race) and two other UAC members - Hugh McFerran (who went on to compete in the race) and Wallace McLeod (Motor Engineering lecturer in Belfast Technical College and motoring correspondent for the Belfast News-Letter).

Both the Belfast Telegraph and Belfast News-Letter published photographs of suitably serious looking people looking at maps with the Telegraph also including a photograph of the hairpin with an arrow showing the direction the race would follow.

Captain Phillips was quoted in all the newspapers as saying that he would recommend issuing a permit. The Northern Whig also reported that he was enthusiastic about the primary purpose of the race - that of encouraging young racing drivers:

* No idea where the reporter got July from.

Above: Officials of the UAC explaining the County Down Trophy Race course to RAC Press Secretary Captain Phillips (third from left). Also in the photograph to the right of Captain Phillips are Fred Rodgers, William Noble and Wallace McLeod. Photo UAC Archive.

"In England, he said, the mountain races at Brooklands and those at Donnington Park have provided opportunities for young English drivers to learn their business, and in the Free State the Phoenix Park races have been invaluable.

Now that the Ulster Automobile Club has taken this step forward, prospective racing drivers of Northern Ireland will be able to meet on much more level terms with their competitors from the other parts of the United Kingdom."

He also added *"the course should give a most interesting race. It has characteristics of a most unusual type and ought to provide first-class experience in the hazards which comprise road racing."*

The RAC Race Permit

The Belfast Telegraph, Belfast News-Letter and Northern Whig all reported between 12 and 27 of April 1934 that the RAC had granted a permit for the County Down Trophy Race. It was granted subject to the following conditions :

- Resurfacing of the short leg (Ballyminetragh Road) and the removal of portions of grass verge in order to make the road slightly wider;
- Warning boards being posted at approaches to the three corners and to indicate undulations;
- At the three corners slip roads to be kept clear for 300 yards to remove the danger to spectators in the event of a corner being overshot;
- No mechanics to be carried in cars;
- The number of competitors limited to twenty;
- Car engine capacity to be under 3,000 cc;
- The course marshalled by police and expert flag marshals;
- The UAC to insure itself and the RAC against any claims arising out of the race and practice and
- Competitors to be covered by insurance.

The County Down Trophy

When the UAC announced back in March that the entrant (not driver) of the winning car would receive the County Down Trophy (and a cash prize of £50) the club had, no doubt, already started making approaches to potential benefactors.

On the 20 April 1934 the Belfast News-Letter reported *"a letter was received yesterday by Captain W J Thompson, honorary secretary of the Ulster Automobile Club from Lord Wakefield of Hythe, intimating that he would be pleased to present a challenge trophy for the 100 miles County Down Race, to be held on the Donaghadee circuit on Saturday 30th June."*

The UAC has a collection of silverware dating back to very beginning of the club but unfortunately it does not include the County Down Trophy. The inscription on the trophy reads:

Ulster Automobile Club
The County Down Trophy
Presented by
LORD WAKEFIELD OF
HYTHE, C.B.E., LL.D
1934

Right: The County Down Trophy. Photo UAC Archives.

A Nationality Problem

The Irish Automobile Club in Dublin, established in 1901 (it gained the Royal prefix much later) was originally responsible for motoring (and motorsport) throughout Ireland. It was affiliated to the Automobile Club of Great Britain and Ireland (which later became the Royal Automobile Club), the overall governing body for the United Kingdom of Great Britain and Ireland.

When the partition of Ireland took place in 1921 the RAC and the RIAC agreed to continue the existing arrangement - the RIAC in Dublin would remain responsible for all of Ireland and stay affiliated to the RAC in London. In 1926 the RIAC relinquished responsibly for Northern Ireland (after much pressure from the North) and in 1927 the link to the RAC in London ended.

Up until 1933 there had been no insurmountable problems preventing drivers from both sides of the Irish border or from Britain competing in local events in either jurisdiction. Indeed given the relatively small numbers of competitors in either part of Ireland, organisers and clubs depended on attracting drivers from all over the Ireland and where possible from Britain. As well as increasing entry numbers it also made the races more interesting for spectators. However in October 1933 there was an amendment to what was referred to in the press as the International Sporting Code which put a spanner in the works.

The motoring correspondent of the Belfast News-Letter was the first to highlight the issue of Irish Free State drivers. competing in the Down Trophy Races in an article published on 20 April 1934:

" The amendment referred to was to the effect that a "national" event is open only to entrants and drivers of the country in which the event is organised. But no doubt the international authority has in mind only such cases as that of

England, France, Germany and other Continental countries. Both the Bray and the County Down Trophy races are "national" events.

It is understood that the matter has been taken up by the Ulster Automobile Club, and that a favourable announcement on the subject is expected within the next day or two. Neither Ulster nor the Irish Free State could possibly be independent in respect of entries for a road race of any magnitude, and it is believed that for the purposes of sport, the two governing bodies - the RAC and the RIAC - are prepared to regard England, Scotland, Wales, the Irish Free State, and Ulster as one country"

An article in the Newtownards Chronicle dated 24 May 1934 refers to a letter Donaghadee Council received from the UAC Hon Secretary W J Thompson:

"The most serious difficulty at present is that the Royal Automobile Club is prepared to only issue a permit for a National Open Competition which will exclude the possibility of entries from the Irish Free State. This is an unfortunate circumstance, as it was hoped that all least six competitors from the Irish Motor Racing Club would have participated in the event."

The RIAC in Dublin, on the other hand, were quite happy for an UAC team to compete in the Bray race on 19 May whereas the RAC in London, as late as the 24 May, still maintained that Irish Free State drivers could not enter the Down Trophy Race!

Some sort of solution was found - drivers from the Irish Free State did, in the end, compete in the Down Trophy Race. In 1935 it became the International Down Trophy Race thereby allowing entries from both parts of Ireland and other nations.

The Down Trophy Race Regulations

The UAC decided at a meeting of the Race Committee on 20 April 1934 to seek permission from Down County Council and Donaghadee Urban Council to hold practising for the Down Trophy Race between 10 am and 12 noon on Thursday the 28 June. All entrants had to take part in the practice to qualify for the race itself on Saturday 30 June.

The Belfast News-Letter (21 April 1934) reported that at the same meeting permission was granted to the BBC to broadcast a running commentary on the event.

It was also announced the prizes would be distributed at a dance held in Donaghadee after the close of the race.

The Northern Whig reported (4 May 1934) that the regulations for the Down Trophy Race had been officially issued by the UAC. The article included the following details:

• The race will be a handicap event, the capabilities of the individual cars and the experience of their drivers being taken into consideration;
• All four wheel cars whose bodies have a minimum of 2 seats and whose engine capacity does not exceed 3,000 cc will be eligible to compete;
• The RAC has limited the number of starters to 20 and the UAC will have to select these if the entries exceed that figure;
• The entrant of the winning car will be the holder of the County Down Trophy (which has been presented by Lord Wakefield of Hythe) and will also receive a replica and £50;
• The second, third and fourth cars will also receive replicas and £25, £10 and £5 respectively;
• The circuit is approximately 3 3/4 miles length and triangular in shape. The roads forming it are the usual first and second class variety, and there are no hills of importance, but many short rises and falls;
• Practising will take place on Thursday, June 28;

- The starting point is about 16 miles from Belfast;
- The entry fees are £3 3s (plus £1 10s insurance premium) until noon on June 2 and £6 6s (with the same insurance premium) until June 16;
- Team entries are 10s 6d per car and £1 1s for the same periods;
- The race is open to all drivers from Great Britain and Northern Ireland and members of recognised automobile clubs in the Irish Free State;
- Mechanics will not be carried.

The article went on to say that the Society of Motor Manufacturers and Traders (SMMT) had granted permission for trade participation and support **PROVIDING** entries were not made by the manufacturers but by or on behalf of local distributors and dealers.

The issue of the race being restricted to UK drivers was still unresolved at this time. The UAC, confident that the matter would be sorted, made no mention of this in the regulations and sent entry forms out to drivers in the Irish Free State.

Cuairt Bhré (Bray) 19 May 1934

Given the similarities between the two races it is no surprise that the press took the opportunity to compare both the races and the organisational skills of the UAC and IMRC.

Bray and Donaghadee are small seaside town on the east coast of Ireland, similar distance from their respective capital cities (Dublin and Belfast) and 1934 was the first time road races were held in either. Both races were run on handicap, the courses were similar in length (less than 4 miles) and run over similar distances (just over 100 miles). There were twenty entrants for the Bray race and, as stated earlier, the Donaghadee race was limited to 20 cars. There were, however, important differences between the races.

 The Cuairt Bhré was a round the houses street race with the start/finish on the mile long seafront (Strand) road. The hotel owners and traders of Bray, by all accounts, recognised the crowd pulling potential of the races including during practice (Thursday 17) and they were prepared (for the most part) to put up with the limited movement around town, helped by the provision of two temporary pedestrian bridges. For the race start the Bray Race Committee used the established practice of lining the cars up on one side of the road pointing towards the middle.

The Down Trophy Race was not a round the houses race - the course was on the edge of Donaghadee and used rural roads with very few houses. The Down Trophy also saw the introduction, for the first time in Ireland, of a grid start (more on this later).

The Cuairt Bhré took place over a month before the Down Trophy and was a great success. The race winner was RBS Le Fanu in a 1994 cc Adler. Eight cars completed the course and three more were still running when the race was declared over. Irish Auto Sport (31 May 1934) reported *"this is an unusually high percentage of reliability for car racing of this type."*

The UAC entered six members: H C McFerran (Bugatti), C G Neill (Bugatti), W T McCalla (Sunbeam), Alan Corry (MG Magna), W R Baird (Riley) and D McMullan (MG Magnette). Only McCalla finished the race.

Trevor McCalla, in the ex-Henry Segrave and Brooklands record holding Grand Prix Sunbeam was scratch and came second (by 2.35 secs), a truly remarkable achievement. He was awarded the Joseph McGrath Cup, £25 and the Fruitfield Cup for the fastest speed for cars exceeding 1100 cc.

The other UAC members did less well. Hugh McFerran crashed at Martello bend. The Alan Corry MG broke down. C G Neill was thrown from his car when it overturned and somersaulted three times at Montore bend. The crash can be seen in the short British Pathé News film of the race.

Irish Auto Sport described the Cuairt Bhré Car race as *"An Exciting Event and Unqualified Success."* The organisation of the race was highly praised. The performance of the UAC teams was considered disappointing more due to bad luck than bad driving, although the pit control work was criticised: *"but all these misfortunes are entirely outweighed by the our recollections of the clever driving of W T McCalla, and the magnificent reception which he received after the race and at the prize distribution."*

Regarding the forthcoming Down Trophy Race the article went on to say to the organisers: "The Cuairt Bhré has set a standard of organisation to the Race Committee which will keep them hard at it in an endeavour to keep their end up. Comparisons may be odious, but they are an incentive to effort."

The UAC had a hard act to follow.

The labours of R J McWhinney

R J McWhinney was the Donaghadee Town Clerk in 1934 and responsible for liaising with the UAC, including attending Race Committee meetings as required and reporting back to both his own Council and Down County Council

Road racing in Northern Ireland prior to 1973 (when very significant changes were made to local government) required at the very least approval for the road closing from the relevant County Council (which was not always granted). The Ards TT came within the area controlled by Down County Council so it was well experienced in dealing with road race organisers. It knew what the benefits were and how much work for councils was involved. Both Donaghadee and Bangor Councils came under the Down County Council umbrella.

In 1934 one of the key considerations for Down County Council was who was going to pay for the road improvements the County Surveyor and the RAC wanted to enable the Down Trophy Race to take place. Agreement was reached with the UAC regarding the apportionment of costs with the local councils responsible for carrying out the work. The Down County Council Finance, Law and Parliamentary Committee dealt with all race related matters.

A Newtownards Chronicle article (24 May 1934) on Down County Council meetings includes an update from R J McWhinney on a meeting he had with the Down Trophy Race Committee and work on getting the roads ready:

"The Committee asked that he should endeavour to secure control of the field at the rectory. He had approached the Church body on the matter, and he did not anticipate any difficulty. The Committee wanted to make the field an official car park or paddock, with the timekeepers box in the corner and the pits along the footpath."

Referring to the hairpin some *"scarifying material had been put on the bank at the corner and the kerbs taken up."* In addition there were plans was to *"roll in"* the kerb at the junction of the Newtownards and Bangor roads and take off *"the nose"* at the corner.

The report went on to say that the Race Committee gave the Clerk the task of asking the people of Donaghadee to contribute the £25 cost of one of the race prizes.

"I do not know whether it was rash or not, continued the Clerk, but I said the Donaghadee people would be very lacking in their duty if they did not realise the importance of the race and raise at least £25. I have three subscription sheets in the town at present, and I think the people will be failing in their duty if they do not raise at least this amount. I am hoping to go round the shopkeepers, hotel keepers and such like, and I am sure that they will realise the importance of the event, and contribute to the fund."

There was precedence for doing this, the people and traders in Bangor contributed every year to the prize money for the Ulster Motor Rally. R J McWhinney did succeed in raising the £25. He was also asked about possible venues in Donaghadee for the planned UAC prize giving and dance and, no doubt, a hundred and one other things.

The 1934 Entries

The Northern Whig ran an article with the following headlines on the 19 June 1934

Co. Down Trophy Race

England, Free State and Ulster

23 ENTRANTS

Forthcoming Motor Thrills at Donaghadee

Included in the article was a list of the 23 entries received by the final 16 June deadline (included in Appendix 3).

It is a list of entrants, not drivers. More often than not the entrant was the driver but not always. For example In the article it states that Montgomery had nominated J W Patterson to drive his Wolseley Hornet.

Missing from the entry list was UAC member and regular competitor C G Neil. He overturned his Bugatti when competing at Bray the previous month and had not yet fully recovered from his injuries, which included several broken ribs. However he volunteered to help as an official.

The maximum number of entrants was limited to twenty, so three entrants could have been held as reserve. The Light Car (29 June 1934) lists only 2 reserve entrants - J McArdle and L Innis.

Race Practice - 28 June 1934

Scrutineering was on Wednesday 27 June at 2 pm in J B Ferguson's, Chichester Street, Belfast. Practice was from 10 am to noon on Thursday 28 June. Spectators had to be in place by 9.30 am.

Hugh McFerran's Bugatti going through the brake test as part of the scrutineering that was carried out in J B Ferguson's garage with Wallace McLeod (third from left) supervising. Photo UAC Archive.

21 cars were expected at the practice (19 confirmed entries plus 2 reserves - McArdle and Innis) . McArdle and Innis did not turn up. I don't know why McArdle did not show but Innis's Morris Minor reportedly was damaged in an accident on the way to the course.

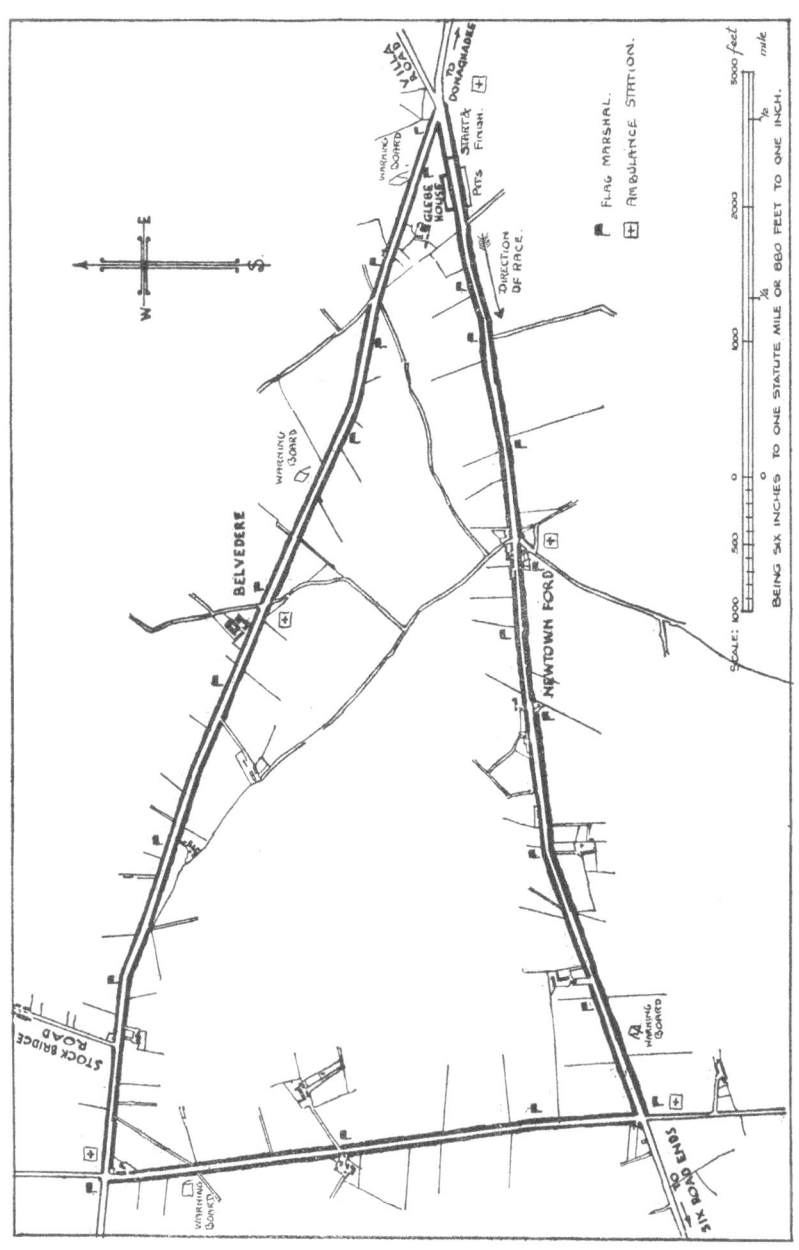

36

The nineteen drivers below took part in the practice:

No	Name	Home	Car
1	W T McCalla	Crossgar	S/C Sunbeam
2	H C McFerran	Belfast	Bugatti
3	W R Baird	Belfast	Riley
4	D C MacLachlan	Cork	Riley
5	W J Kavanagh	Dublin	Riley
6	D Mackenzie	Dublin	Riley
7	P Donnelly	Dublin	Riley
8	"A Corry"	Belfast	MG Magna
9	W Sulivan	Belfast	Sullivan Special s/c
11	A R Finlay	Bangor	MG Magna
12*	David Yule	Dublin	S/C Austin
14	E J Wilkinson	Belfast	Singer
15	J R Hodge	London	Singer
16	W F Ayrton	Belfast	MG
17	Flight Lieut L R Briggs	Belfast	MG
18	J McGrattan	Bangor	MG
19	M H Fleming	Belfast	MG
20	J W Patterson	Ballymena	Wolseley Hornet
21	F W Earney	N'Ards	Amilcar

*number not confirmed

There were three cars with drivers who were not the entrants:

J W Patterson, Wolseley Hornet - entered by W M D Montgomery;

P Donnelly, Riley, entered by T O'Shaunessy and

"Alan Corry" MG Magna, entered by H C McFerran.

It was noted in all the papers that "Alan Corry" was not the real name of the driver. It was in fact Lloyd Cowdy - more about Lloyd later.

An article in the Belfast News-Letter (22 June 1934) stated *"the course was reported to be in splendid condition after its treatment with tar and screenings……..The most acute corner, the Donaghadee hairpin, is not expected to provide very much excitement as it is so sharp that it could not be taken except at very low speeds. Everything points to Angus Corner round which the cars will travel to join the inland Bangor-Donaghadee road as the most tricky, and there will probably be some excitement for spectators there.*

By far the best vantage point, however, will be the car park enclosure adjacent to the pits and starting point, for here the nerve centre of the race organisation will be situated. Loud speakers will be provided, by means of which spectators will be kept in touch with events round the 3 3/4 mile course. An admission charge of 2s 6d per head will be charged."

I assume the 6d on top of the two shillings was to cover the Entertainment Tax - see next page.

COUNTY DOWN TROPHY
MOTOR ROAD RACE

30TH JUNE, 1934

SALE OF ENTERTAINMENTS DUTY STAMPS

In connection with the County Down trophy Motor race, it may not be generally known that Entertainment tax is chargeable not only on payments to special stands but on all payments (above 6d made to anyone for permission to view the Race from a field, car, window, roof or balcony).

The Tax is paid by gumming an adhesive Entertainment Duty Stamp on the admission ticket and tearing both at the time of arrival so that the proprietor (or ticket checker) and the person admitted each retain half. Those that do not want to go to the expense of printing their own tickets can obtain printed Government stamped tickets free of cost on paying the value of the stamps.

Adhesive stamps are on sale at the GPO Belfast, and at the post offices in Bangor and Newtownards, whilst Government stamped tickets can be obtained from the sales Office, HM Stationery Office, 80 Chichester Street, Belfast.

Explanatory Leaflets showing the rates of duty payable can be obtained on application to the Ministry of Finance, Stormont, Belfast.

TWO CRASHES IN RACE PRACTICE
(BELFAST NEWS-LETTER 29 June 1934)

There were two crashes during practice, thankfully neither very serious, and it is no surprise that these featured in many newspaper headlines the next day - for example the above headline in the Belfast News-Letter.

On his first lap David Yule crashed at McCoubrey's Corner, the first on the course. The Belfast News-Letter report stated:

"The flag marshal at the corner said that the car was approaching the corner far out on the left-hand side of the road. The driver braked and went into a speed skid, with the rear wheels trailing in the gutter.

When it was almost on the corner the car struck the hedge and, scattering officials and spectators in all directions, turned two somersaults and came to rest in the slip road. The driver was thrown out opposite the officials box, his crash helmet flew off when he was mid-air.

Fortunately both a doctor and an ambulance were stationed at the corner, and Yule, who was able to walk, was at once rushed to the Newtownards hospital. He had a bad cut over one eye, which had temporarily closed, and abrasions to hands, knees, and chest. That night he was stated to be fairly comfortable, though suffering from shock.

The car is extensively but not really seriously damaged. All four wheels are out of true, and the windscreens are smashed, and the tail badly dented. Yule was visited by friends after practising. He attributes the crash to the fact that the shock-absorbers were too tightly adjusted."

J W Patterson (Wolseley Hornet) crashed on his second lap, about half a mile from the start line. According to the Belfast

News-Letter there were no eye witnesses "but on his return to the pits Patterson said that he had been forced to swerve to miss another competitor and finished up underneath his car in the ditch." According to the Northern Whig (29 June 1934) Patterson *"was greatly relieved when a squad of marshals sprinted up and released me."* He walked back to the pits and was treated by Dr H F Northey, Chief Medical Officer. He was fortunate to get away with just a broken collarbone.

Above: J W Patterson (far right) walking away from the crashed Wolseley Hornet. Photo with thanks to the British Newspaper Archive.

There was a rumour that F W Earney had crashed the Amilcar but that proved to be unfounded. Near the end of practice A R Finlay, driving a MG Magna, drove up a bank at the first corner. The axle and one wheel were damaged but he was unhurt.

Surprisingly few cars suffered serious mechanical problems. W R (Bobby) Baird blew the engine on his Riley on the second lap. The engine had only been fitted the day before practice and Baird was not best pleased. He was able to get the Riley running again in time for the race on Saturday morning.

The Ayrton MG broke a rocker arm when being driven by reserve driver N F Gordon but by that stage both drivers had qualified and the car was fixed in time for Saturday.

The Singer driven by E J Wilkinson survived practice but the gearbox seized afterwards. The car had to be driven home in third gear. The gearbox problem was fixed in time for Saturday.

Seventeen cars successfully qualified for the race. The Belfast News-Letter published the top eleven best lap times:

Name	Car	Time	M P H
H C McFerran	Bugatti	3 min 25 secs	66.92
W T McCalla	Sunbeam	3 min 28 secs	65.96
J R Hodge	Singer	3 min 32 secs	64.71
"A Corry"	MG Magna	3 min 34 secs	64.11
W J Kavanagh	Riley	3 min 50 secs	59.65
D M Mackenzie	Riley	3 min 52 secs	59.13
D C MacLachlan	Riley	3 min 53 secs	58.33
W R Baird	Riley	3 min 56 secs	58.13
W Sullivan	Sulivan Special	3 min 57 secs	57.89
A R Finlay	MG Magna	3 min 57 secs	57.89
L R Briggs	MG Midget	3 min 57 secs	57.89

The remaining four drivers had lap times over 4 minutes.

Practice Results 1934

A Belfast News-Letter reporter (possibly Wallace McLeod) included an interesting analysis of the practice results in an article dated 29 June 1934.

The reporter compared the fastest lap (3 min 32 secs) by J R Hodge, in the stream-lined 972 cc Le Mans Singer against the fastest lap (3 min 28 secs) by Trevor McCalla in the 1,992 cc supercharged Grand Prix Sunbeam. Based on this and the difference on handicap (McCalla was on *"scratch"* meaning he had to drive the full distance) in theory at least the Singer could finish 13 minutes ahead of the"big supercharged Sunbeam."

J R Hodge, 972 cc Singer Le Mans. Photo Michael Wylie collection.

The reporter continued the comparison between the two cars:

"This is, of course, pure presumption, it is expected that McCalla cannot improve on yesterday's times, and from the point of view of mechanical durability his would be one of the last cars in race to blow up.

In the case of Hodge's car, this machine is obviously very highly tuned. He experienced the effect of the terrific strain on the plugs during practice, and he made several stops to change to new sets. A very highly tuned engine is not so likely to stand up to the gruelling pace as an engine which runs at slower speeds."

It is interesting that the fast lap set by A R Finlay in the 1,087 cc MG Magna and the Flight Lieutenant L R Briggs in the 847 cc MG Midget were the same (3 min 57 secs). Handicap races usually work to the advantage of cars with smaller engines which could work in Briggs' favour.

The Briggs' MG Midget was considered to have *"a very desirable combination of tune and durability"* and *"the car seems to be one of the best prepared for the race."* Again the smaller engine was seen as working in its favour in terms of handicap.

Hugh McFerran in the Bugatti put in the fastest lap (3 min 25 secs) and the reporter regarded the car as *"more suitable for the course than that of McCalla."* However according to reports McCalla never exceeded 3,500 revs during practice - the Sunbeam had a lot more power available if he had the skill and was brave enough to use it.

D C MacLachlan's 1098 cc Riley with its works engine was regarded as having *"something up its sleeve."* His fastest lap time of 3 min 53 secs *"must not be taken as an indication of his race speed."*

Bravely the reporter gave his (heavily caveated) prediction of how the race might turn out:

"L R Briggs, "Alan Corry" and W T McCalla might occupy the first three places in that order, with D MacLachlan and H C McFerran the dangers."

In his report the Northern Whig correspondent (29 June 1934) broadly agreed although, referring to the fast speeds set in practice by Huge McFerran and Trevor McCalla he commented:

"However these fast speeds by no means indicated the rosiness of the big cars' chances, as the practice tends to show that the handicap erred on the side of favouring the less experienced drivers."

Without committing himself, the reporter went on to write *"generally the opinion is that the winner will be found among men like J R Hodge, the London driver of an extremely modern-looking Le Mans 972cc Singer, Flight Lieutenant L R Briggs, of Belfast, on a 847 cc MG or D C MacLachlan, the skilful Cork driver of one of the five 1,089 cc Rileys in the race."*

I wonder if the Belfast News-Letter and Northern Whig motoring correspondents had a friendly bet on who came closest to getting the result right. The Belfast Telegraph motoring correspondent in his report (29 June 1934) played it safe and did not venture any opinion on who might win.

J McGrattan 18 (MG) leading L R Briggs 17 (MG) on the Bangor Road . Photo with thanks to the British Newspaper Archive.

Trevor McCalla 1 (Sunbeam) about to overtake A R Ayrton 16 (MG) on the Bangor Road. Photo with thanks to the British Newspaper Archive.

P Donnelly 7 (Riley) leading J McGrattan 18 (MG) at Angus corner. Photo with thanks to the British Newspaper Archive.

The caption for the above photograph in the Belfast News-Letter states T O'Shaunessy (Riley). However although O'Shaunessy entered the Riley, P Donnelly was the driver who qualified and took part in the race. I think it is more likely to be Donnelly behind the wheel but I am happy to be corrected.

BELFAST AND COUNTY DOWN RAILWAY.

SPECIAL EVENTS AND CHEAP FARES
TO COUNTY DOWN RESORTS
ON SATURDAY, 30th JUNE

TO DONAGHADEE [FOR COUNTY DOWN TROPHY RACE] RETURN FARE **1/6**

VIEW THE ROAD RACE FROM VANTAGE POINTS AT DONAGHADEE.
TRAINS from BELFAST at :—
10.30 a.m., 12.10 p.m., 1.30 p.m., 2.5 p.m. (Special), 2.15 p.m., 3.20 p.m.

PASSENGERS can take advantage of the

BELFAST, BANGOR AND DONAGHADEE CIRCULAR TOUR
to View the ROAD RACE, travelling out from Belfast by Rail to Bangor, Motor Coach to Donaghadee, and Rail Donaghadee to Belfast, or vice versa.

INCLUSIVE FARE
RAIL AND MOTOR **2/-**

TO BANGOR   -   -   -   RETURN FARE **1/-**

[VISIT OF H.M.S. "NELSON" AND "CRESCENT" TO BANGOR BAY]

TO NEWCASTLE (for the Mountains of Mourne) **AFTERNOON TRIP**

Leave Belfast 2.30 p.m.   RETURN FARE **1/6**
Returning 8.45 p.m.

TO HOLYWOOD (for REGATTA and AQUATIC SPORTS), Frequent Rail and Bus Service.

Tickets valid for Return on day of issue.   W. F. MINNIS, General Manager.

Advertisement in the Belfast daily newspapers in the days leading up to the race.

48

Programme Pirates and a Grid Start

The race was originally to start at 3 pm on Saturday June 30 1934 but the time was changed to 3.15 pm to *"facilitate police arrangements."* (Northern Whig 26 June 1934) In the same article it stated that *"pirate programmes for the race are already appearing, but the race can only be followed properly from the official programme, published by the UAC at 6d."*

Official programmes were (and can still be) an important source of revenue for race organisers and the pirates apparently had been selling advertising space in their programmes. Going by the newspaper report, the problem of pirate programmes was widespread and not restricted to only motorsport events. It may explain why the daily papers printed details of the 17 drivers, their cars and the handicaps but not the drivers race numbers.

A number of the newspapers highlighted the use of a grid (or massed) start for the race and some included details of the grid positions. The Belfast News-Letter in the morning edition (30 June 1934) referred to *"a starting system, which is new to Ireland, but which is employed in Grand Prix events on the continent, will be used. By this method drivers with the fastest times are lined up in front and the slower times behind."*

 The Northern Whig (29 June 1934) claimed it was the first time a grid start was used in Ireland and that it should *"make a most spectacular start. There will be no disappointments - as sometimes occur in the TT of "crack" drivers losing valuable time getting "dumb" engines at the start, for the grid will line up with engines running and first gear engaged by their drivers awaiting the fall of the starter's flag."*

The following lists of drivers, cars, handicaps as well as their respective grid positions was printed in the Belfast News-Letter (30 June 1934)

Drivers, Cars and Handicaps.

Driver	Car	CC	H'cap (laps) credit
W T McCalla	Sunbeam s/c	1992	0
H C McFerran	Bugatti	1990	1
W R Baird	Riley	1089	1
D C MacLachlan	Riley	1089	1
W J Kavanagh	Riley	1089	2
D M Mackenzie	Riley	1089	2
P Donnelly	Riley	1089	2
"A Corry"	MG	1087	2
W Sullivan	Sullivan Special s/c	732	2
A R Finlay	MG	1087	3
E J Wilkinson	Singer	972	4
J R Hodge	Singer	972	4
W F Ayrton	MG	1250	4
L R Briggs	MG	847	5
J McGrattan	MG	847	5
M H Fleming	MG	847	5
F W Earney	Amilcar	1087	5

The race was 30 laps and the handicap worked on the basis of credit laps. First to finish won but how many laps you had to drive to finish depended on your handicap.

For example W T McCalla (Sunbeam) was "scratch". He had zero credit laps and therefore had to drive the full 30 laps to finish. By contrast L R Briggs (MG) had five credit laps - he had to drive only 25 laps to finish.

The grid positions were as follows:

	2 McFerran		1 McCalla	
15 Hodge		8 "Corry"		5 Kavanagh
	6 Mackenzie		4 MacLachlan	
3 Baird		9 Sullivan		11 Finlay
	17 Briggs		7 Donnelly	
16 Ayrton		18 McGrattan		14 Wilkinson
	19 Fleming		21 Earney	

There were three reserve drivers:
N F Gordon (reserve for W F Ayrton);
J S C Cupples (reserve for L R Briggs) and
J Thompson (reserve for J McGrattan)

Road Closing

The roads were to be closed at 2.30 pm by A H Wilkinson in a Riley. Once the roads were closed motorists could still reach Donaghadee, either by the coast road from Bangor or the Moss Road from Six Road Ends where RAC signposts were erected to guide traffic on the police approved routes.

A H Wilkinson closing the roads in his Riley. Photo with thanks to the British Newspaper Archive.

Donaghadee 30 June 1934 - Officials

Details of race officials are often not included in accounts of motor races. Most were (and still are today) volunteers. For the record their details are included in the appendices in the order they were listed by the UAC.

There are 45 officials listed and that does not include all the flag marshals and police. It does include no less than 12 doctors. There were five ambulance posts around the course including the one near the start/finish. This would have allowed for two doctors at each ambulance post plus the Chief Medical officer and one other at race control.

The number of officials involved is a good indication of (a) how much work was involved in staging the event and (b) the determination of the UAC that it should be a success.

The 1934 Drivers

The following are a combination of information printed in the Belfast News-Letter, UAC Monthly Review, The Bray Motor Races with some contributions of my own. The drivers are listed in race number order (where known).

1: William Trevor McCalla, Crossgar, Supercharged Grand Prix Sunbeam

McCalla *"has in his Sunbeam by far the fastest car in the race. This two litre machine holds three international Class E records but it naturally will not show its true speed to-day. McCalla is the scratch man, and has a good deal of time to make up. He will actually have to travel something over 114 miles but there is very little question of his not lasting the course. He is relying on his acceleration and brakes for a win, and has something "up his sleeve" on his practice laps. He will be very interesting to watch and ranks amongst the best drivers in the race."* (Belfast News-Letter)

"McCalla, drove a magnificent race at Bray last month in this car - starting from the very back in the handicap and finishing second, being only beaten by the limit car by less than 3 seconds." (UAC Monthly Review)

Above: Trevor McCalla in the paddock at Bray, May 1934. Photo UAC Archive.

2: H C McFerran, Belfast, Grand Prix Bugatti

"H C McFerran, Belfast, has the distinction of returning the fastest lap time on Thursday. McFerran is a competent driver , and he should do well with his two litre Grand Prix Bugatti. This car was doing well at Bray last month when it crashed, and given a clear run it should figure high up in the list this evening. McFerran is allowed one lap from McCalla, although his car is really more suitable than the Sunbeam for this course." (Belfast News-Letter)

"McFerran's successes in hill-climbs are many, and date back for a number of years. In 1932 he gained second place at the Phoenix Park Senior Fifty Miles Race, driving a "Magna" on that occasion." (UAC Monthly Review).

H C McFerran entered a second car, an MG Magna, driven by "A Corry".

3: W R Baird, Belfast, Brooklands Riley

"W R Baird, who finished sixth in the 1933 Tourist Trophy Race, and secured the Clery Trophy for the fastest time in the 1100 cc Class at Phoenix Park in the same year, will drive a Brooklands Riley." (UAC Monthly Review)

He entered the Bray Race in 1934 and during practice, in an attempt to avoid a skidding Trevor McCalla, overshot the course, went through the gateway of the Bray Head Hotel and came to a stop at its front door.

Despite qualifying he did not compete in the race itself on medical advice (severe chill). He would have been the handicap scratch man. (Source: Robin McCullagh, the Bray Motor Races)

The only son of Sir William Baird, owner of the Belfast Telegraph who, apparently, did not entirely approve of William Robert's (Bobby) motor racing exploits - whether it was the danger, the expense or both I don't know. This does not appear to have deterred Bobby in the slightest.

A popular figure, Bobby Baird raced all over Ireland and England including Brooklands, and was one of Northern Ireland's most gifted drivers.

LEFT: Bobby Baird on the left and Hugh McFerran in the middle at Bray in May 1934. Photo UAC Archive.

4: D C MacLachlan, Cork, Riley

The Belfast News-Letter and UAC Monthly Review profiles give very different impressions of this driver:

"D C MacLachlan, of Cork, is at the present moment a "dark horse." He is the veteran driver of the race, from the point of view of experience, and whatever happens, he will probably keep going steadily throughout. He is not a man for hair-raising speed, but knows the limit of both his engine and chassis, and keeps nicely inside those limits.

His best practice time of 3 min 53 secs is no indication of his race speed, and ensures him a fairly good place at the start." (Belfast News-Letter)

"D C MacLachlan will drive the Riley with which he raced in the 1931 Irish Grand Prix and in the 1932 and 1933 IMRC Races in Phoenix Park. His latest success was in securing his Class Prize at the IMRC Bray "round-the-Houses" race last month." (UAC Monthly Review)

MacLachlan finished 5th overall at the Bray and was awarded the McGuirk Cup for the fastest car under 1100 cc. (Source: Robin McCullagh, The Bray Motor Races)

5: W J Kavanagh, Dublin, Brooklands Riley

"W J Kavanagh, of Dublin, will drive his recently purchased Brooklands Riley. He has not yet raced this car, but will be well remembered for his exploits with the supercharged Austin with which he collected a number of prizes in university events, and finished second in the Junior Phoenix Park Race last year with an average speed of 65.5 mph." (UAC Monthly Review)

He was a non starter at the Bray - the car he entered had been damaged the week before in a event in London and the Bray officials refused to allow him to change his car to the Riley as it was after the closing date for entries. (Source: Robin McCullagh, The Bray Motor Races)

6: D M Mackenzie, Dublin, Riley

"D M Mackenzie, another Dublin driver, will compete in a Riley to which he has made a number of alterations after the "Freddy Dixon" manner. He also completed at Bray." (UAC Monthly Review)

The reference to Mackenzie competing at Bray may be wrong - I can find no mention of him competing and he is not listed as one of the finishers.

7: P Donnelly, Ireland, Brooklands Riley

The Brooklands Riley driven by P Donnelly; the car was entered by T O'Shaunessy.

I have no other information on P Donnelly. The Brooklands Riley, VC 834, still survives to this day.

8: "A Corry", MG L Type Magna

The use of false names was not unusual at this time but the true identity of "A Corry" was no mystery in local motorsport circles.

He was Lloyd Cowdy, only son of (Frances) Charles and Hazel Cowdy. His great grandfather established Anthony Cowdy & Sons, Linen Manufacturers and Bleachers around 1870.

Charles Cowdy competed in the Royal North of Ireland Yacht Club motor meet and hill climb at Cultra in 1910 in a Talbot. He came second in Class 2.

The Cultra hill climbs were a fairly genteel affair with nothing approaching the speeds attained at hill climbs in the 1930s and Charles prohibited his son Lloyd from competing in any form of motor sport - hence the false name. The same prohibition did not extend to his sister Hilda who competed under her real name, for example at Craigantlet Hill Climb.

Lloyd drove an MG Magna in the Phoenix Park Races in 1933 and at the Bray Races in 1934 (where he retired on the 14th lap with back axle problems).

9: W Sullivan, Belfast, Supercharged Sullivan Special

" W Sullivan, who has many successes to his credit, and is, perhaps the most experienced driver entered, will compete in a supercharged "Sullivan Special" Morris." (UAC Monthly Review)

The writer may have felt that was all he needed to say. Billy Sullivan competed in almost every hill climb and motor race in Northern Ireland including the TT and would have been well known to UAC members. He was seldom out of the newspapers and advertisements for his business, the Belfast Car Laundry Ltd appeared regularly in the newspapers as well as in the UAC Monthly Review.

Billy Sullivan in the paddock, Donaghadee.
Photo with thanks to the British Newspaper Archive.

11: A R Finlay, Bangor, MG L Type Magna

All the UAC Monthly Review had to say about Alfie R Finlay
was that he was from Bangor and would be driving an L Type
MG Magna.

14: E J Wilkinson, Belfast, Singer Le Mans

"E J Wilkinson will drive a Le Mans 972 cc Singer entered by
his father, Mr A H Wilkinson. Well known in hill climbing
competitions Mr Wilkinson has usually driven Riley cars in
previous events." (UAC Monthly Review)

Associated with Leslie Porter Ltd, 24/28 Great Victoria Street,
Belfast, agents for Riley and Singer, Ernie Wilkinson first
competed in 1930 at Craigantlet Hill Climb. Usually entered by
his father he subsequently competed at Ballybannon, Croft,
and Red Brae hill climbs. He was the winner of Class 7
(handicap, open to all cars) at Ballybannon in June 1933
driving a March Special Riley.

**Ernie Wilkinson, Singer, exiting the hairpin during practice.
Photo Michael Wylie collection.**

15: J R Hodge, London, Singer Le Mans

"J R Hodge is the "speed merchant" of to-day. His splendid practice laps of 3 min 32 secs on Thursday in his spectacular streamlined Le Mans Singer overshadowed the performance of the other drivers. Although this machine is not by any means the fastest in the race, it has the great advantage of a 4 lap handicap. It may prove too highly tuned for the work it will be called upon to do. J R Hodge is a Londoner. He drove at Craigantlet Hill Climb last year, and can always be relied on to go fast." (Belfast News-Letter)

The UAC commented that he also had considerable success in Car Dirt-Track Racing events.

**J R Hodge, Singer Le Mans, in the pits at Donaghadee.
Photo Johnson collection.**

16: W F Ayrton, Northern Ireland, MG F Type Magna

"W F Ayrton, well known in local competition circles, will make his racing debut with his F Type "Magna" the engine capacity of which is 1,250 cc, as compared to the 1,087 cc of the L Type." (UAC Monthly Review)
Ayrton competed in Class 3 (cars, other than racing cars, up to 1,500cc and supercharged cars up to 1100 cc) at Ballybannon in June 1933 in his MG Magna. He came third with a time of 1 min 15 secs.

17: Flight Lieutenant L R Briggs, Greenisland, MG Midget

" L R Briggs is favourite for the race in several quarters. The local driver is known to be steady, his practice laps show him to be fast. His MG Midget is a well-tuned reliable little car that is very unlikely to give any trouble mechanically. On handicap, Briggs is one of the limit men, receiving five laps from McCalla, who will have to pass him once every twenty minutes - a difficult task. Briggs and his little car will be watched with great interest. The superstitious will notice that he is carrying the same number under which Nuvolari won the last TT." (Belfast News-Letter)

"Briggs has entered his very fast MG Midget which he drove at Phoenix Park, and with which he won the 860 cc Class for unsupercharged cars at Craigantlet in 1933." (UAC Monthly Review)

18: J McGrattan, Bangor, MG Midget

The UAC Monthly Review had little to say about J McGrattan (spelt McGratten in the Review) other than to say he was a newcomer to racing and drove an MG Midget. He does not appear to have competed previously at hill climbs or speed events in Northern Ireland

Flight Lieutenant Briggs, MG Midget, in the pits at Donaghadee.
Photo Johnson collection.

19: Malcolm H Fleming, Belfast, MG Midget

Another driver the UAC Monthly Review had little information on other than mistakenly saying he was from Bangor (he was from Belfast) and drove an MG Midget.

M H Fleming competed at Ballybannon Hill Climb in June 1933 in classes 1 and 7 in an MG Midget. He got through to the second round in Class 1 where he was beaten by J S C Cupples in another MG Midget. Cupples went on to win the class.

**Malcolm Fleming (19) leading P Donnelly (7) and J McGrattan (18) round the Donaghadee hairpin during practice.
Photo author's collection.**

21: F W Earney, Newtownards, Amilcar

" F W Earney, of Newtownards, has entered the only Amilcar in the race. Mr Earney has been an Amilcar enthusiast since 1926, having competed since that year at Magilligan sand-races and at hill-climbs in cars of this make." (UAC Monthly Review)

He competed at least nine times between 1926 and 1933, at the Ballybannon, Craigantlet and Croft hill climbs as well as at the Magilligan Speed trials and races. He always competed in an Amilcar, often against cars with much bigger engines.

Going by his competition entries he owned at least three different Amilcars - 1,074 cc, 1,087 cc and 1500 cc models.

F W Earney, 1,087 cc Amilcar on his last lap at the Magilligan Strand races October 1927.
Photo with thanks to the British Newspaper Archive.

DANCE AND PRIZE DISTRIBUTION

"On the evening of the day of the race, a dance will be held in Caproni's Cafe Miramar, Seacliffe Road, Bangor, Co Down, at which the prizes will be presented to the successful competitors by Lady Dunleath.

The price of admission to the dance will be 3 shillings per person.

Further particulars and tickets for enclosure and Car park can be obtained from the Ulster Automobile Club Office, 65 Chichester St Belfast - Telephone: Belfast 1480."

(Ulster Automobile Club Monthly Review, May 1934)

Caproni owned a number of different establishments in the Bangor area used by the UAC for dances and prize givings. Whatever the merits of the Cafe Miramar may have been, it was in Bangor, not Donaghadee!

Bangor. **CAPRONI** Phone 45

CO. DOWN TROPHY RACE DANCE
TO-NIGHT.
PRESENTATION OF PRIZES BY LADY DUNLEATH
Cabaret by Lena King
Admission 3/-.
DANCING EVERY WEDNESDAY AND SATURDAY.

Race Day - 30 June 1934

"All roads led to the new circuit and as the closing hour approached one was reminded of the London-Epson Road on Derby Day. Cars of all makes, sizes and ages made a continuous procession to the official car parks, and these were intertwined with every other conceivable mode of conveyance, and a large contingent on "Shank's Mare."…..the race was held in the most perfect weather it would be possible to imagine, perhaps slightly too perfect, for as the race wore on the corners oozed a little (also the more exposed spectators)." (Spectator 7 July 1934)

The Spectator estimated that 50,000 came to watch. *"By 3.10 pm the roads were completely clear, everybody had settled down to their spy-holes, and the cars, with engines running, were in position for the massed start - the fastest cars were in front - McFerran's Bugatti and McCalla's Sunbeam, once the property of the late Sir Henry Segrave.*

The rest of the field yelped and snarled at their heels and gave the impression that they were only waiting for the flag to drop, and then fall on the Bug and Sunbeam and tear them to pieces.

But nothing of the sort happened, for the two leading cars shot off like twin streaks of lightning, as a matter of fact so did everyone else, barring Donnelly's Riley which made distinctly sluggish start."

The UAC report on the race also mentions that the starters got away well expect Donnelly who*"did not quite get into his stride with the others."*

The grid start. McFerran (2) in front of McCalla (1), with Hodge (15) and "A Corry" (8) behind.
Photo with thanks to the British Newspaper Archive.

The first cars, McCalla (Sunbeam), McFerran (Bugatti), Hodge (Le Mans Singer), Kavanagh and MacLachlan (both Rileys) arrived back at the start much quicker than the crowd expected. McCalla did his first lap in 3 mins 32 secs (64.66 mph) and all the others were within a few seconds of him.

On the third lap McCalla and Baird (Riley) both beat McFerran's practice lap time of 3 mins 25 secs. The Spectator described Baird *"driving with a delightful abandon reminiscent of the famous Freddie Dixon's style. His cornering was very snappy indeed."*

The Spectator reporter was not quite sure what to make of Hodge's Le Mans Singer describing it as *"a very queer looking animal this - or was it a bird - with a long skinny pointed tail which positively flapped up and down when he went over the bumps. A couple of humps added to its tail and it would have looked like one of the famous denizens of Lough Ness."*

The Spectator noted the *"thrilling duel: between the English driver Hodge, and the "Bangor hope" Finlay driving an MG Magna"*in the early part of the race. *"Lap after lap the little monster and the Magna fought each other, one gaining a few seconds and then the other, and on one occasion, ignoring the man with the flag, they took the corner simultaneously."*

"Bangor hope" Alfie Finlay (11) and London driver J R Hodge (15) coming out of the hairpin.
Photo Michael Wylie collection.

The support for the exhaust pipe on McFerran's Bugatti gave problems almost from the start. On the fourth lap he ended up pushing the black Bugatti to the pits and several minutes were spent making a repair before he rejoined the race. He *'drove like a demon to make up his lost time."* (Spectator) F W Earney, Amilcar, retired on the fifth lap (reason unknown). P Donnelly, Riley, managed nine laps before retiring (reason unknown) while the engine in the "A Corry" MG Magna lasted 15 laps (sheared camshaft drive).

Pat Donnelly (7) Riley and J R Hodge (15) Singer coming out of the hairpin. Photo Michael Wylie collection.

Between mechanical problems and putting his Riley in the ditch at McCoubreys corner, Cork driver D C MacLachlan, had a difficult race. Undeterred he kept going to the end.

It was warm work, according to the Spectator, *"many drivers decided to put comfort before personal safety and removed their crash helmets."*

By the half way point (15 laps covered) the first six positions by handicap were as follows:

1	J Hodge	Le Mans Singer	+1 min 32 secs
2	L R Briggs	MG Midget	+ 1 min 29 secs
3	W Baird	Riley	-1 sec
4	A R Finlay	MG Magna	- 12secs
5	"A Corry"	MG Magna	- 24 secs
6	W T McCalla	Sunbeam	- 30 secs

Ayrton (16) MG leading Wilkinson (14) Singer and Fleming (19) MG out of the hairpin. Photo Michael Wylie collection.

Bobby Baird, in the red Riley was the fastest man on the corners and was getting faster with every lap. The Northern Whig referred to his *"hurricane driving"* and he twice equalled the best lap time set in practice and went on to establish a new lap record of 3 min 23 secs (67.57 mph). He worked his way up to second position and it looked like he might win the race. Alas it did not last and on his 18th lap the Riley engine blew up. He had to walk back to the pits where *"he got a great ovation from the crowd"* (Northern Whig) and joined the spectators watching the race.

It was at about this time that Hodge hit a hedge at McCoubrey's corner. He was unhurt and was able to pull the car out of the hedge and limp round to the pits to change a buckled wheel before rejoining the fray. According to reports Hodge was markedly slower after that and gradually lost position through *"cautious cornering"*.

J R Hodge, Le Mans Singer, goes into a hedge. Photo UAC Archive.

Right: L R Briggs (17), MG, was leading up until the 23rd lap. Photo Michael Wylie collection

At the end of twentieth lap L R Briggs was in the lead on handicap and J R Hodge had dropped well behind. McCalla was catching up. The top six on handicap now were:

1	L R Briggs	MG Midget	+ 2 min 47 secs
2	W T McCalla	Sunbeam	- 16 secs
3	A R Finlay	MG Magna	- 26 secs
4	W F Ayrton	MG Magna	- 1 min 21 secs
5	W J Kavanagh	Riley	- 2 min 30 secs
6	B Sullivan	Sullivan Special	- 2 min 44 secs

On lap 22 the record for the course for was broken for the last time. The record had been alternatively held by Baird and McFerran but now McCalla set a new record with a time of 3 mins 15 secs (70.34 mph).

The Briggs,"little car was going round very fast and quiet." (Spectator), and was still in front and almost a lap ahead of fellow MG drivers, Aryton and Finlay. Unfortunately on the 23rd lap a big end bearing went, the engine lost oil pressure, and he was out. It was a gallant effort.

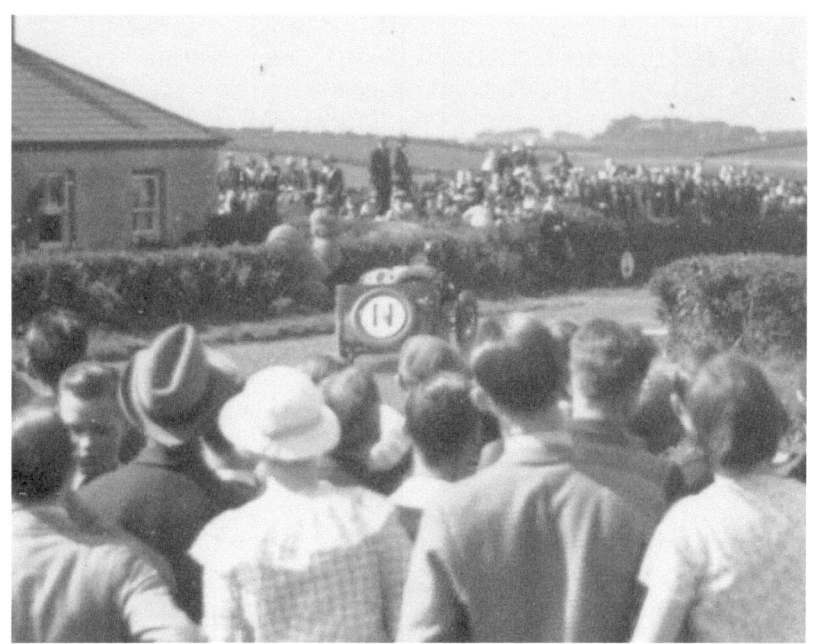

Spectators enjoying great weather and a great motor race. Bangor man Alfie Finlay (MG) at McCoubrey's corner. Photo Johnson collection.

W J Kavanagh also retired on the 23rd lap, for reasons unknown, after nursing his Riley back to the pits. McCalla was still speeding up and by the 25th lap was in first place on handicap.

McFerran retired on the 26th lap after stopping on the side of the course to try yet again to fix the black Bugatti's exhaust - in the end he took it off and threw it in a ditch!

After that McCalla's position was safe. On the 27th lap he passed Alfie Finlay and it was clear to the crowd, handicap or not, who was winning. From then on there was no catching the young Crossgar driver in the car the Northern Whig named "The Green Bullet". He came in victorious, quickly followed by two MG drivers - A R Finlay (the Bangor hope) and W F Ayrton. The remaining seven cars finished within 14 minutes.

McCalla, Sunbeam, takes the chequered flag. Photo UAC Archive.

The 1934 Results

Name	Car No	H'cap Laps	Time H.M.S.	Speed (MPH)
1st W T McCalla, 2 litre Sunbeam	1	0	1h 42m 19s	67.14
2nd A R Finlay, L-type MG Magna	11	3	1h 42m 55s	59.98
3rd W R Ayrton, F-type MG Magna	16	4	1h 43m 47s	57.27
4th E J Wilkinson, Le Mans Singer	14	4	1h 47m 2s	55.53
5th W Sullivan, Sullivan Special Morris Minor	9	2	1h 48m 0s	59.27
6th J R Hodge, Le Mans Singer	15	4	1h 48m 24s	54.83
7th J McGrattan, MG Midget	18	5	1h 50m 37s	51.67
8th D C MacLachlan, 1,089 cc Riley	4	2	1h 52m 33s	58.91
9th D M Mackenzie 1,089 cc Riley	3	3	1h 55m 45s	55.22
10th M H Fleming MG Midget	19	5	1 h 55m 54s	49.31

Also competed: H C McFerran (1,990 cc Bugatti) 26 laps; W J Kavanagh (1,089 cc Riley) & L R Briggs (847 cc MG) 23 laps; W R Baird (1,089 cc Riley) 18 laps; "Alan Corry" (L-type Magna) 15 laps; P Donnelly (1,089 cc Riley) 9 laps; F W Earney (1,087 cc Amilcar) 5 laps.

Trevor McCalla, winner of the County Down Trophy, with his sister (Mrs Hanson). Photo Michael Wylie collection.

"As I mentioned earlier the winning car was once the property of the late Sir Henry Segrave; that great driver would be glad to see his old car winning races long after he ceased to drive.

And although we have lost Segrave, Birkin and many others, we must look to the County Down Trophy to provide us with our future Segraves and Birkins!" (Spectator 7 July 1934)

After the Race - everybody happy (almost)

The event was heralded in all the papers as a great success and it appears only one complaint, about the prize giving, managed to make it into the papers. More on that later.

The UAC was delighted and, I am sure, greatly relieved that all went well. Nevertheless they were aware of the limitations of the Donaghadee course. The enclosure was not ideally placed - the cars had to slow down to almost walking pace to go around the hairpin, not the most exciting thing to watch. However there was no other possible location for the enclosure. Spectators dotted around the course had to contend with high hedges and the few gaps allowing a good view were filled very early - one spectator brought a periscope!

It was also clear that the course did not allow most of the cars to get up to any great speed, especially coming out of the hairpin: *"even the winning Sunbeam looked almost painfully slow in picking up, certainly far below what was expected from a supercharged two-litre engine…..some of the smaller cars seen at this point seemed as if merely out for an airing, so slowly did they get away from the corner."* (UAC Monthly Review).

To my mind the biggest drawback of the Donaghadee course was the restriction to only twenty cars imposed by the RAC.

Despite being a great success 1934 was the first and last time the County Down Trophy Race was held on the Donaghadee course. It was however the start of a series of motor road races in Northern Ireland that continued right up to 1955.

Colonel Lindsay Lloyd on Success of Race

Lady Dunleath presented the prizes at a celebration dance at Caproni's Cafe Miramar, Bangor.

To McCalla went the County Down trophy - a perpetual cup presented by Viscount Wakefield - a replica, and £50, presented by the UAC.

To Finlay went a replica and £25 presented by the townspeople of Donaghadee. Ayrton won a replica and £10, presented by Mr William Noble, Chairman of the UAC.

Mr A H Wilkinson, as the entrant of the car driven by his son, E J Wilkinson, received the cash prize of £5, presented by himself, and a replica.

Colonel Lindsay Lloyd, of the RAC, after thanking Lady Dunleath for having distributed the prizes, warmly congratulated the UAC on the success of the new race. He paid tribute to Northern Ireland for having arranged so satisfactorily that race, which was of the greatest value in giving what he would call the younger competitors a chance to try their hands at "the most fascinating amusement and great sport of motor racing." If they had not such places for beginners in the sport there would be little chance of getting anyone to compete in the great races such as the RAC Tourist Trophy in Ulster.

Ulster was fortunate in having a club such as the UAC to organise the County Down Trophy Race, which he hoped, would be the first of a long series.

The dance attracted a large attendance and a clever cabaret was given by the pupils of Miss Lena King.

Angry from Donaghadee

The race was over, the winners congratulated and the prizes distributed. The UAC could relax and a crowd of happy competitors, officials, friends and family danced the night away in Caproni's. But you can't please everyone and after the party had ended at least one Donaghadee resident put pen to paper and wrote to the newspapers venting their displeasure. This appeared in the Spectator:

"To raise £25 in Donaghadee, to upset business in Donaghadee on a Saturday, and then present Donaghadee prizes in Bangor is an example of UAC HUMOUR that Donaghadee can't SEE or ENJOY. At any rate it deserves a laurel wreath for TACTLESSNESS."

The writer went on to suggest the Donaghadee ratepayers did not want another UAC organised race in the district.

The Spectator (14 July) published the response from the Donaghadee Town Clerk, R J McWhinney. He confirmed that he was at the meeting when the prize giving was being discussed and was asked about possible venues in Donaghadee. The only venue big enough was the Railway Pavilion and McWhinney confirmed that the Committee did inspect it. There two serious problems with this venue, there was no catering and no orchestra! The UAC would have to pay for both to be brought in and the Club was worried that they would lose money, *"on the other hand the Club was free from financial worry by holding the dance in Bangor. An orchestra was there in addition to a staff adequate to cope with the catering."*

McWhinney also stated that, as far as he could tell, the race had been very popular with ratepayers and most wanted a similar event next year.

What the reaction was in Donaghadee when they discovered the 1935 race was going to be held in Bangor I do not know.

The 1935 County Down Trophy Race

"The Ulster Automobile Club has received intimation from the Royal Automobile Club that the County Down Trophy Race has been granted international status. Saturday, 22nd June has been allotted for the 1935 race." (Belfast News-Letter 19 October 1934)

A new course for 1935

Although the race had already gained international status three months earlier, in January 1935 the Ulster Automobile Club (UAC) was still trying to finalise the route of a course to replace Donaghadee.

The UAC wanted a longer race for 1935; up to 150 miles. This was more about making the race more exciting to watch than anything else. As suggested by the Northern Whig correspondent "SUPERCHARGER" in March 1934 a longer course would mean at least some of the cars would need to re-fuel plus more cars would probably need to come in for repairs. Other aims included getting a course where there would be no limit on engine capacity or the number of cars.

Captain Phillips from the RAC had accompanied UAC officials to inspect several possible courses, for example one course which included the streets of Bangor and nearby Ballyholme. All but one proved unsuitable for various (not specified) reasons but by the end of January a new course was approved by the RAC. Immediately the Club confirmed that it was working with Bangor Borough Council to deliver a 150 mile "round the houses" race which would include the seaside town of Bangor. The new 5 3/4 mile long course was described by the UAC as follows:

"The start, pits, grandstand, and scoreboard will be at the wide stretch of road opposite Bangor Railway station. From here the cars follow the main Bangor to Belfast Road where after a short distance of narrow road the course soon becomes 35 feet wide.

About three quarters of a mile from the start there is an easy gradient, and after this there is nearly one mile of straight road with a falling gradient to the first real corner on the course at Clandeboye Post Office. On this straight the faster cars will be doing well over one hundred miles per hour and the corner will require careful judgement, as it can only be safety taken at sixty miles per hour.

From here to Clandeboye Cross Roads is about one-third of a mile and then the cars will come to the slowest corner on the course, which will bring their speed down to twenty-five miles per hour. The road between here and Crawfordsburn is straight but rather narrow, and at the present moment is the worst part of the road in terms of road surface.

The corner at the end of this straight is awkward, as the route lies downhill for quite a considerable distance before the actual corner itself is reached and has a safe maximum speed of about fifty-five miles per hour.

From Crawfordsburn into Bangor the roads winds and abounds with fast bends on which a skilful driver will be able to gain seconds on his less experienced competitors, and there is a very spectacular bump over the railway bridge[3] where the fastest cars will probably leave the road for a period.

After the railway bridge is passed right down to the Queen's Parade the course is downhill, and this part of the course should undoubtably be the most popular from a spectators point of view. There is an extremely fast bend on to the Parade and drivers who are travelling at too high a speed here may find themselves uncomfortably near the sea wall.

The corner at the end of the Parade into Main Street is reasonably fast, as the road is wide at this point, and from here a short rise and a wide piece of concrete road takes the competitors back to the start.

---

[3] Bangor West railway bridge

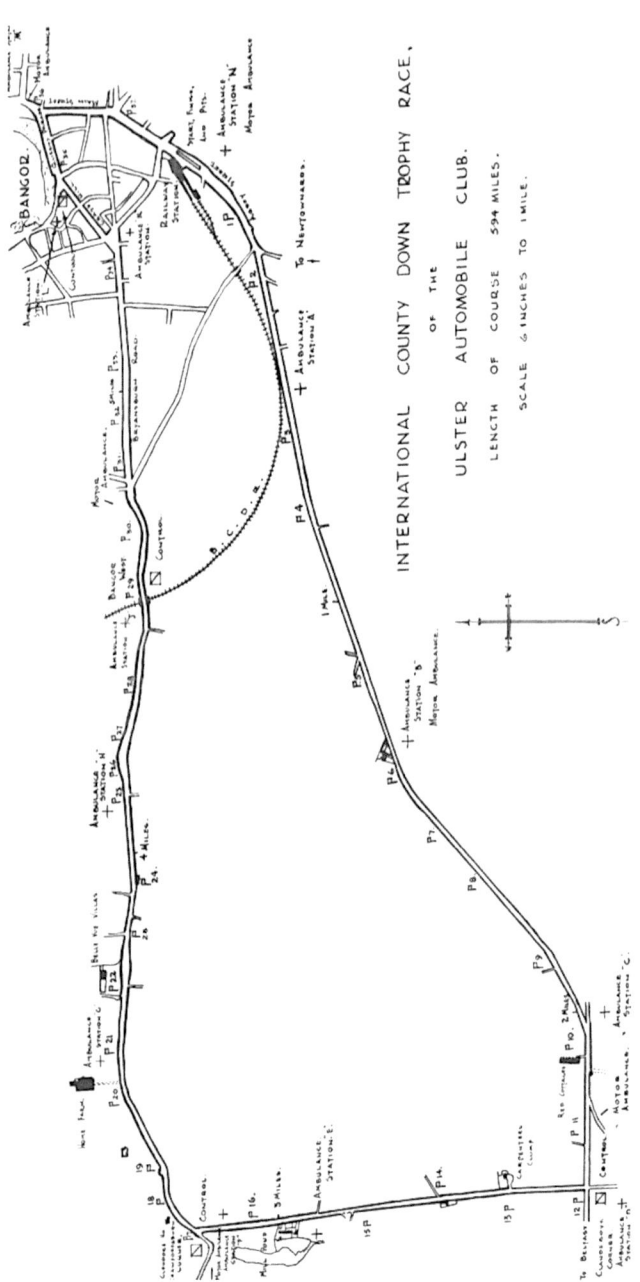

INTERNATIONAL COUNTY DOWN TROPHY RACE,

OF THE

ULSTER AUTOMOBILE CLUB.

LENGTH OF COURSE 5¾ MILES.

SCALE 6 INCHES TO 1 MILE.

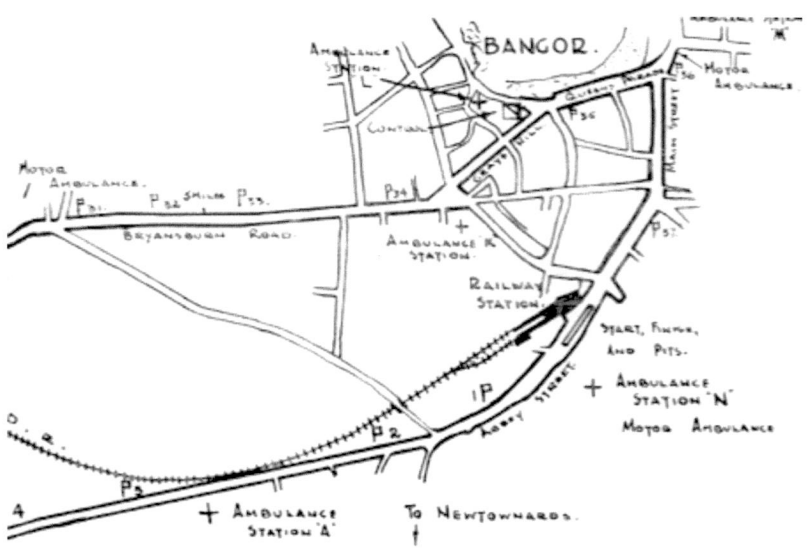

Left: The official course map. Above: Bangor town section.

The length of the circuit is five and three-quarters miles and the full distance of the race for the scratch cars will be 25 laps, which gives 149 1/2 miles."

The following appeared in The Light Car 15 February 1935:

"The County Down road race, run over a course near Donaghadee last year, is to take place in Bangor this season ….. the suggested five mile circuit is as follows: Start Abbey Street, along Belfast Road to Clandeboye cross-roads, turn north to Crawfordsburn, along Crawfordsburn Road, Bryansburn Road, Gray's Hill, Queen's Parade, Main Street and back to Abbey Street.

I suppose that means something to Bangorians but it's Chinese logarithms to me."

"Abbey Street, Bangor, starting point of this year's race for the Down Trophy. The race will also finish at this point, which provides long wide straight where high speeds should be witnessed." (UAC Monthly Review). Photo UAC Archive.

The finish line for the UAC Ulster Motor Rally was also in Abbey Street, Bangor.

Photos UAC Archive and with thanks to the British Newspaper Archive.

Both pictures show the first significant corner on the course at Clandeboye Cross Roads and were taken looking towards Bangor.

"Outside the town the course provides fine straight stretches. Above is the approach to Clandeboye Cross Roads where the corner (on left) leads to Crawfordsburn." UAC Monthly Review

"The turn at Crawfordsburn, one of the most intricate corners on the course." Photo UAC Archive.

Crawfordsburn Road heading towards the Bryansburn Road and then Bangor.
Photo with thanks to the British Newspaper Archive.

Top left: Looking from Bangor West railway bridge along the Bryansburn Road towards Bangor. Photo with thanks to the British Newspaper Archive.

Bottom left: Looking back towards Bangor West railway bridge. Photo taken during practice 1936. Photo Johnson collection

Below shows the junction of Gray's Hill and Queen's Parade. At the end of Queen's Parade the cars turned right and uphill into Main Street. Once they crested the top of Main Street it was straight on to Abbey Street and the start/finish. UAC Monthly Review.

THE INTERNATIONAL COUNTY DOWN TROPHY RACE.—
QUEEN'S PARADE, WHERE RESIDENTS AND VISITORS WILL HAVE A FINE VANTAGE POINT AS THE CARS COME DOWN GRAY'S HILL AND ALONG THE PROMENADE TO MAIN STREET CORNER.

The excitement builds

The daily papers and the motoring press picked up on the regulations when they came out in February. The race would consist of 25 laps of the 5.94 mile course (total distance 148.5 miles). Entries were limited to 40 cars (twice the limit for Donaghadee) and cars could have any type of body and use any grade of fuel. Engines could not exceed five litres.

With its "international" status the 1935 event caught the attention of drivers both near and far (including North America). The UAC issued the following to the local papers to try and generate excitement:

"The club has received enquires from Signor Giro Ferrari, of Genoa, who has asked for copies of the regulations. He also stated in his letter that if he came he would enter either a 2,600 cc Monza Alfa Romeo or a 1,100 cc Maserati or a special Fiat, bringing with him Signor Battilana to drive.

Rumours have also been current that Austin Dobson will have use of a 1934 Monoposto Alfa-Romeo in place of his 2,600 cc Monza model of last year…….Lord De Clifford is also preparing a special Lagonda-Rapier for this race and there is a promise of an entry of three Adlers, these being cars that did so well in Free State Races last year. There is a certain entry of a single seater supercharged Magnette, and there will be a large local entry, including Bugattis, MGs, Singers and Rileys."

Two legs of the course had to be completely resurfaced.The UAC estimated that, when the work was completed, *"the slowest cars should be able to lap at 60 mph while the majority should be averaging very nearly 80 mph"*, much quicker than Donaghadee in 1934 when the fastest lap, 70.34 mph, was set by Trevor McCalla in the Grand Prix Sunbeam.

Prize Money

The newspapers were always keen to publish the prize money for events and, at a time when there were very few works teams, the amount of money on offer certainly could help attract drivers from outside Northern Ireland.

First prize to the entrant of the winning car (not the driver) this year would receive the County Down Trophy and £100 presented by the townspeople of Bangor.

The entrant of the second placed car would receive a replica of the trophy plus £50 presented by the Licensed Traders of Bangor.

The entrant of the third placed car would receive a replica trophy plus £25 presented by Mr E Caproni.

The entrant of the fourth placed car would receive a replica trophy plus £10 presented by the Motor Traders of Bangor.

In addition there was a team prize of £15 15s (15 guineas) and everybody completing the course within 20 minutes of the winner would receive a souvenir award.

The cash prizes were much more generous than the year before due to the very considerable support from the people and businesses in Bangor!

Bangor Motor Sports Committee

The UAC held the Ulster Motor Rally finish in Bangor since it started in 1931 and received generous support from the Council. In his role as Mayor of Bangor, Councillor Walter Malcolm, was elected Vice President of the club in 1934.

Timed to coincide with the UAC announcement of the new County Down Trophy Race course, a press release was issued by the Council with details of a meeting held on 30 January 1935 in the Park Pavilion, Bangor and presided over by Walter Malcolm. At the meeting the Bangor Motor Sports Committee was appointed. Mayor Malcolm made the following statement:

"The race would be organised and run under the auspices of the Ulster Automobile Club and the Bangor Motor Sports Committee" The Committee would "carry out details incidental to the raising of funds and other matters connected with the race."

Holding the Down Trophy Race was a major undertaking with an estimated cost of £500, including the £185 prize money the people and traders in Bangor were committed to providing. There were at least two roads that needed resurfacing, temporary pedestrian bridges to be erected at Abbey Street and Gray's Hill and a host of other things.

Walter Malcolm justified the effort and expense on the grounds that with *"the easy access to the town by rail and bus from Belfast, it was easily conceivable that there might be 100,000 people in Bangor that day. Even if the average expenditure in town by visitors was only 6d per head, it would represent the sum of £2,500 left in town. The raising of the necessary funds should be regarded as an investment."*

Not every Councillor supported the races - Ronald Douglas, a motorist himself, objected on safety grounds pointing out that motor fatalities were increasing. In response the *"Mayor argued that the great efficiency of modern cars had been largely brought about by the exacting tests of races."* Other councillors also said that the people of Bangor had no enthusiasm for the race. However, when it came to a vote, Douglas was the only person dissenting.

In response to concerns about possible losses, Bangor Council made it clear, not least to ratepayers, the financial success or failure of the race would decide if was to be held annually. In the event of a loss the arrangement negotiated with the UAC limited the Council's liability to a maximum of £50.

The Bangor Motor Sports Committee was based in Bangor Town Hall and was chaired by the Mayor of Bangor. It had two secretaries, a treasurer (who was also the organiser) and twenty-two members made up of councillors and local businessmen - details in Appendix 4.

The Committee contacted by letter businesses and residents identified as possible financial supporters. The following are examples of the letters that went out to businesses asking for their contribution.

In addition to the support of the Bangor Motor Sport Committee, the UAC were also able to borrow *"barricading materials and bridges"* from the Ulster TT Race Committee.

Bangor Council later granted permission for the erection of the bridges under the supervision of the Council surveyor.

BANGOR MOTOR SPORTS COMMITTEE

PHONE: BANGOR 134.

Chairman: WALTER MALCOLM, ESQ.

Joint Hon. Secretaries: R. M. MOORE AND T. B. GRAHAM.

Hon. Organiser and Treasurer: H. ROGERS.

Town Hall,

Bangor,

Co. Down.

30th May, 1935.

Dear Sir,

The date of the Co. Down Trophy Race
(Bangor) is fast approaching and preliminary
expenditure has to be provided for.

The Committee would esteem it a favour
if you would remit your promised subscription
to the Hon. Treasurer (Mr. Rogers) by return.
Cheques should be made payable to the Bangor
Motor Sports Committee.

A receipt will be sent to you, and your
promised subscription will be announced in this
week's issue of the "Spectator".

Yours faithfully,
R.M.MOORE, Hon.Secretary.
H.ROGERS, Hon.Treasurer.

BANGOR MOTOR SPORTS COMMITTEE

PHONE: BANGOR 134.

Chairman: WALTER MALCOLM, Esq.

Joint Hon. Secretaries: R. M. MOORE AND T. B. GRAHAM.

Hon. Organiser and Treasurer: H. ROGERS.

Town Hall,
Bangor,
Co. Down.

6th June, 1935.

Dear Sir or Madam,

International Co.Down Trophy Race for Motor Cars.
Saturday, 22nd June, at 3.15 p.m.
Practice - Thursday, 20th June, 3 to 5 p.m.

Arrangements for holding the above event are nearing completion, which, given fine weather, will undoubtedly mean an influx of many thousands of visitors to Bangor, many of whom will remain in the town during the evening.

At the outset, some of the sixteen local Licensed Traders undertook to provide the Second Prize of £50.

In consultation with your representative on the Committee, the Houses have been graded, and what is considered a fair basis for contributions, varying from £5 to £2, has been reached.

The suggested contribution from your House is £

Some of the Houses have already paid sums upwards to £5, and some of the other traders have contributed larger amounts.

Money is now urgently needed to meet heavy, preliminary expenses, and we shall be glad if you will let us have your subscription.

Your contribution should be looked upon as an investment, for such it is bound to be, having in mind the increased turnover on the two days, especially on the Saturday.

The Trade contribution has already been acknowledged in the Press, and a list of individual subscriptions will be published in the "Spectator" in due course.

Your remittance by return will be much appreciated by the Committee.

Yours faithfully,
R.M.MOORE, ⎱
T.B.GRAHAM, ⎰ Joint Hon. Secretaries.
H.ROGERS,   Hon. Treasurer.

99

The 1935 Entries

As in previous events there were early and late entry fees.

Entry forms became available in early March 1935. The fee for entries received up to noon on May 2 was £3 3s per car. The fee for entries received after that and before noon 10 June was double (£6 6s per car).

In addition there was an insurance charge of £2 per competitor to cover third party risks.

Thirty entries were received - twenty five entries before 2 May and a further five (at double cost) by the 10 June deadline.

The five entries at double cost were Sir Herbert Austin (Austin), J Chambers (Riley), S C Collier (MG), A Dobson (Alfa-Romeo) and N G Robinson (Wolseley).

There were four more Bugattis entered in 1935 compared to 1934, two more MGs and, for the first time, two Alfa Romeos plus two supercharged Austin single seaters.

Only one Riley car was entered compared to five the previous year.

Notably missing from the entry list was "A Corry", real name, Lloyd Cowdy. This may possibly be explained by a cable the UAC received containing notice of the marriage at Mafeking, South Africa on the 17 May of Lloyd Cowdy to Miss Eleanor T Bailey.

A full list of all the 1935 entries is in Appendix 3. Please note although there were 30 entries the race numbers go up to 31 - number 13 was not used.

Putting the standards in position for the pedestrian bridge at Grey's Hill, Bangor. There was a second bridge erected at Main Street. The bridges were on loan from the Ulster TT Race Committee. Photo with thanks to the British Newspaper Archive.

Workmen marking out the site for the grandstand and enclosure in Abbey Street. Photo with thanks to the British Newspaper Archive.

Race Practice - Thursday 20 June 1935

Belfast News-Letter 20 June 1935:

"Official practising will take place to-day at Bangor for the International County Down Trophy car race on Saturday, arranged by the Ulster Automobile Club. The roads forming the course will be closed from 2.30 pm until 5.30 pm.

Intending spectators are advised to secure their enclosure tickets, of which only a limited number are on sale. There are two enclosures, one opposite the pits and the railway station, at which seats will be available, and one at Queen's parade for promenading only.

Tickets may be obtained from at the Ulster Automobile Club, 65 Chichester Street; Messrs Leahy, Kelly and Leahy; the Athletic Stores; and at Bangor.

Loud speakers will be installed at both enclosures and the progress of the race around the course can be followed. By purchasing an official programme, the only one with complete and accurate information, spectators will be making a direct contribution to the cost of the race.

Residents in Bangor and district, and particularly those in the vicinity of the course, should see that their domestic pets are kept in house, or under strict control, during practice on Thursday and the race on Saturday. The organisers of the race will greatly appreciate the co-operation of the public in their efforts to avoid any accident however slight."

Scrutineering was on Wednesday afternoon (19 June) and Thursday morning in J B Ferguson's garage in Belfast.

A Carr, Lagonda, undergoing scrutineering at the J B Ferguson garage in Belfast. Photo UAC Archive

Practice was between 3 pm and 5 pm and each driver had to complete at least three laps at or above a minimum speed specified by the timekeepers.

The weather on Thursday afternoon was perfect and there were large crowds behind the barriers in the town and hundreds more around the course. The road was closed by A H Wilkinson in a Riley (registration CZ 6611). Wilkinson also brought Royal Ulster Constabulary County Inspector Regan on a tour of the course to examine how the police on duty had been deployed!

Although thirty entries were received, two did not turn up for practice - G F A Manby-Colegrave and G. Abecassis.

According to the Belfast News-Letter, during practice Luis Fontés lapped at an average speed of 78.32 mph in his Alfa Romeo and *"his car was by no means flat out for the entire circuit."*

Fontés was quoted as saying that the course was more difficult than the 'round the houses' course at the Isle of Man. *"The stretch between Clandeboye and Crawfordsburn is very tricky and will require careful driving. I think the race will be very exciting."*

No crashes were reported during practice although F H ffrench Davis (FIAT) managed to go through a hedge at Clandeboye but got away with a few scratches and a buckled wheel. A jay-walking dog at Main Street had a narrow escape.

Number 31, F Smyth (Ford) from Belfast was the only driver to fail to qualify.

Five reserve drivers also qualified: G Rand, W H Wilson, C L Goodacre, J E Gibson and J C Bartlett.

Race Practice 1935 - Lap Times

The following list of best lap times was printed in the Belfast News-Letter on 21 June 1935:

Driver	Car	Min	Secs	MPH
Luis Fontés	Alfa Romeo s/c	4	33	78.32
Austin Dobson	Alfa Romeo s/c	4	39	76.63
L P Driscoll	Austin s/c	4	51	73.47
W Sullivan	Bugatti	4	55	72.48
I F Connell	Vale s/c	4	58	71.75
H C McFerran	Bugatti	5	1	71.03
W T McCalla	Sunbeam s/c	5	1	71.03
W R Baird	MG Midget s/c	5	2	70.80
C G Neill	Bugatti	5	2	70.80
P Dwyer	Bugatti	5	5	70.10
S C Collier	MG Magnette s/c	5	10	68.97
J Chambers	Riley	5	18	67.24
J Wesley Shaw	Triumph s/c	5	19	67.03
E Griffiths Hughes	Frazer Nash	5	20	66.82
L R Briggs	MG Midget	5	29	64.99
D Taylor	Bugatti	5	30	64.79
R A Scott	MG	5	30	64.79
H W Furey	MG Magnette	5	32	64.40
John Hodge	MG Magnette	5	32	64.40

K N Hutchinson	Ford	5	36	63.63
F H ffrench Davis	FIAT	5	37	63.44
W F Ayrton	MG Magnette	5	58	59.72
W A Bartlett	C & T Special	6	28	55.10
N G Robinson	Wolseley	6	44	52.92

Lap times were not printed for four drivers:

A Carr (Lagonda),
M H Fleming (MG),
J McGrattan (MG) and
F Smyth (Ford)

F Smyth was the only one who failed to qualify

The pits in Abbey Street during practice: Photo Author's collection.

J Chambers (Riley) leading J W Shaw (Triumph) down Gray's Hill during practice. Photo with thanks to the British Newspaper Archive.

Luis Fontés, Alfa Romeo, at Bangor West railway bridge during practice. Photo Author's collection.
Saturday 22 June 1935

On the Wireless.

To-day's B.B.C. Programmes.

NORTHERN IRELAND.

10.15 a.m., Daily Service. 10.30, Time and Weather. 10.45, Scottish. 11.45, Northern. 12.15 p.m., Regional. 1.0, National. 2.0, B.B.C. Northern Ireland Orchestra; leader, Philip Whiteway; conductor, E. Godfrey Brown. 3.0, Running commentary by John V. H. Couper and Henry W. M'Mullan on the International County Down Trophy Race at Bangor. 3.45, National. 5.0, The International County Down Trophy Race commentary continued. 5.30, Children. 6.0, First News, including Weather Forecast, Bulletin for Farmers, and Northern Ireland news. 6.30, Gramophone Records: Orchestras of the World. 6.45, Echoes of Ulster. 7.0, Regional. 9.15, Weather Forecast for Northern Ireland; News from Road and Track; a review of Motor Sport, by Mr. Brian Lewis. 9.35, Gramophone Records. 10.0, Time, Weather, and News. 10.10—12.0, Regional.

The five entries that did not race

There were thirty entries (see Appendix 3) but only twenty-five cars started the race.

The five who did not race were:

G F A Manby-Cosgrave, race number 3, MG Magnette, did not attend practice.
G Abecassis, race number 20, Austin s/c, did not attend practice.
F Smyth, race number 31, Ford, stripped the engine timing wheels on the 3rd lap during practice and did not qualify.
W R Baird, race number 8, MG, qualified but did not start the race itself. His car was involved in an incident when driven by a mechanic on the Friday and a replacement could not be made ready in time.
N G Robinson, race number 27, Wolseley, qualified in practice but *"blew the engine in a most comprehensive manner."* He was unable to repair it in time for the race.

Fourteen of the drivers were from Northern Ireland, eight from England, two from the Irish Free State and one, Sam Collier, from the USA (New York).

The race, as it did in 1934, involved a grid (or massed) start, with positions based on practice times and the number of laps to be completed based on the handicap applied. The handicaps were in credit laps, not time, so the fastest (scratch) cars at the front of the grid had to complete twenty-five laps to finish whereas the slowest cars at the back had six (credit) laps less to drive.

Four teams entered including one from the Irish Motor Racing club (IRMC):

Team A	Race No	Driver	Car
	4	W T McCalla	Sunbeam s/c
	19	W F Ayrton	MG Magnette
	25	L R Briggs	MG Midget
Team B	**Race No**	**Driver**	**Car**
	5	I F Connell	Vale s/c
	15	E Griffiths Hughes	Frazer Nash
	23	J R Hodge	MG Magnette
Team C	**Race No**	**Driver**	**Car**
	7	H C McFerran	Bugatti
	11	C G Neill	Bugatti
	12	W Sullivan	Bugatti
Team D	**Race No**	**Driver**	**Car**
IMRC	2	A Dobson	Alfa Romeo
IMRC	3	G F A Manby-Colegrave*	MG Magnette
IMRC	10	P Dwyer	Bugatti

* G F A Manby-Colegrave put in an entry but did not turn up for practice and therefore did not qualify.

The 1935 Drivers

A number of publications as well as the official programme, published short descriptions of the drivers and cars. The following has been put together from various sources. Drivers dates of birth are included if known.

1. Luis Fontés, Alfa Romeo, 2,336 cc s/c.

Luis Fontés, (born 26 December 1912, Reading, England) was the son of a Brazilian shipping magnate. He took up motor racing in 1933, initially racing MGs. He later bought John Cobb's Alfa Romeo Monza and in 1935, driving this car (painted green), he won the International Trophy at Brooklands (6 May) and the Mannin Moar on the Isle of Man (31 May). On the 15 June, just a week before the County Down Trophy Race, Fontés, with John Hindmarsh, won the Le Mans 24 hour race in a works Lagonda Rapide.

His Alfa Romeo was reported to be the most successful car in the County Down Trophy Race and nearly the fastest.

The Luis Fontés Alfa Romeo. Photo Dermot Johnson Snr.

2. Austin Dobson, Alfa Romeo, 2,600 cc s/c.

Austin Dobson (born 19 August 1912, Surrey, England) and his brother Arthur were both motor racing drivers. In addition to the Alfa Romeo Monza he also owned the ex-Sir Henry Birkin Maserati Tipo 8C.

The UAC regarded the Alfa Romeo Monza as the fastest car in the Down Trophy race: *"and on the bonnet it bears the infamous Ferrari shield which puts it in a plane above other cars. This is a wonderful machine and its acceleration has to be seen to be believed. It was in this car that Mr Austin Dobson broke the Phoenix Park lap record last year at 94.7 mph, and he also finished second in the Leinster Trophy Race at an average speed of 72.2 mph."*

It is not surprising that Fontés and Dobson made up the front row of the grid.

Austin Dobson, Alfa Romeo. Photo Dermot Johnson Snr.

4. W T McCalla, Sunbeam, 1,992 cc s/c.

Former Campbell College Belfast pupil, William Trevor McCalla (born 16 November 1904, Strandtown, Belfast) first started competing in 1926 at Ballybannon Hill Climb in an Amilcar. He came second (to Victor Ferguson in an Austin 7) and might have won had he not run out of petrol halfway up the hill.

He later drove a Riley at Craigantlet and also a 3 litre Bentley. The Bentley was entered for the IMRC races in Phoenix Park in 1932 but Trevor failed to finish due to a fractured petrol pipe.

He came second at Ballybannon in 1933 driving a 4 1/2 litre Bentley and later that year won the Noble Trophy (for the second time) at Craigantlet.

He bought the ex-Sir Henry Segrave 1924 Grand Prix Sunbeam in 1934 and in that car won the first County Down Trophy Race in Donaghadee.

5. I F Connell, Vale, 1,496cc s/c.

Ian Ferguson Connell (Cambridge, born 15 October 1913 Singapore) started racing in a D Type MG Midget at Montlhéry while taking a year out before going to Caius College Cambridge. In 1934 he bought an Austin Ulster which he raced in the Brooklands Mountain handicap and later that year won a Glacier Cup in the Alpine Trial driving a Singer Nine Le Mans.

The Vale with its 1,496 cc Coventry Climax OHV engine and Centric supercharger may have been built to order by the Vale Motor Company for Connell in 1935. He drove the car in the 500 mile race at Brooklands but the car retired with a cracked cylinder head. It was subsequently fitted with a more effective radiator.

The UAC described Connell in the County Down Trophy Race programme as having *"plenty of both racing and hill climbing experience and was second in the Long Handicap at Brooklands on the 10th inst with this car."*

6. S C Collier, MG Magnette, 1.087 cc s/c.

Samuel (Sam) Carnes Collier (New York, born 14 May 1912) with his two brothers, Miles and Barron Junior, made MG racing history in the USA in the 1930s.

In 1934 Sam, along with his brother Miles, travelled to Europe looking for race cars. They came back with a 1929 Riley Brooklands, a six cylinder L Type MG Magna (for their other brother) AND negotiated a deal with Cecil Kimber to become the first official USA MG importers. The cars were sold through a foreign car dealership in Manhattan belonging to their friend and fellow racer George Rand.

Collier returned to Europe in 1935 and included the Down Trophy Race in his itinerary. Both he and his reserve driver George Rand qualified. Very little was written about Collier in the Northern Ireland papers or monthly magazines other than he was the entrant and driver of an MG Magnette, and was from New York. At least one paper reported that he was travelling to Europe on the RMS Aquitania. I assume George Rand travelled with him.

This particular MG Magnette (K3001) was originally owned by Whitney Straight and later bought and raced by Richard Seaman. Sam Collier bought the car in 1935 and the County Down Trophy was the first race he competed in as part of his European tour that year. (Source: The Hawke History of MMM Competition Cars)

Opposite page: The Vale Special, Abbey Street, Bangor 1935. Photo Johnson collection.

7. H C Mc Ferran, Bugatti Type 35 GP, 1,990 cc.

Hugh McFerran (Belfast) was a member of the UAC Committee and an enthusiastic competitor in both hill climbs and road races.

The UAC Monthly Review describes this car as a full GP Bugatti. It was *"a recent acquisition, and, although untried on Irish road races, it has a very fine record at Brooklands. It is one of the best of this type of car produced, of which there are very few, and the driver is confidently expected to extract every ounce of speed out of it."*

Bugatti, Abbey Street, Bangor. Photo Bugatti Trust.

9. L P Driscoll, Austin, 747 cc s/c.

Sir Herbert Austin was the entrant of the 747 cc side valve supercharged single seater Austin driven by L P (Pat) Driscoll.

 Leonard Patrick (Pat) Driscoll, born 1900 Middlesex, England, initially raced motorcycles before moving on to cars. He is described in the UAC Monthly review as *"the well known Brooklands driver"* and the car *"has been specially built for racing alone, is extremely light and the engine develops tremendous power. The body is very like that of the GP Mercedes"*

In the County Down Trophy programme it adds that Pat Driscoll *"is the holder of the 750 cc Mountain Circuit lap record at Brooklands"* and the car *"has won its class at Shelsley Walsh"*

Pat Driscoll in the pits at Bangor surrounded by young autograph hunters. Photo Johnson collection.

10. P Dwyer, Bugatti Type 57, 3,255 cc.

Philip Dwyer (Cahir, Co Tipperary,Ireland) was one of the two
drivers from the Irish Free State and the UAC and Belfast
press knew very little about him.

The car was a Type 57 sports car with the original body
replaced by a lightweight one for racing.

The first road race for both the car and driver was at Bray on
18 May 1935 and the car *impressed everyone with its
acceleration, road handling and silence."* Dwyer finished in 9th
place.

**Philip Dwyer, Bugatti, Main Street Bangor.
Photo Johnson collection.**

11. C G Neill, Bugatti Type 35 GP, 1,990 cc.

C G (Gordon) Neill (Belfast) was a stalwart member of the UAC and, many years later, would become club secretary and responsible for, among other things, both the Ulster Trophy and later RAC TT races at Dundrod.

" This car is the one he has been using for the last 2 years and the best effort accomplished was the winning of the Cosgrave Cup at the 1933 Phoenix Park meeting, at 78.3 mph. He has since competed without success in several of the Irish races and hill climbs." (UAC Monthly Review)

As mentioned previously he was unable to compete in the first County Down Trophy race at Donaghadee as he was recovering from injuries as a result of a spectacular crash in the 1934 Bray race. He competed at Bray again in 1935 as a member of the UAC team where, due to a mix up in pit signals he failed to finish within 15 minutes of the winner.

12. W Sullivan, Bugatti Type 35A GP, 1,990 cc.

W (Billy) Sullivan (Killyleagh, Co Down) was described by the UAC as *"the most experienced road racing driver in Ireland and there are very few drivers in England that could be called his equal. He has competed in nearly every TT race as well as the Isle of Man events and the Irish Grand Prix."*

Sullivan got the car from Hugh McFerran. It is the one McFerran drove in the 1934 County Down Trophy Race and in the 1935 Leinster Trophy Race when he came 5th.

Billy Sullivan's Belfast Car Laundry business looked after the cars for Hugh McFerran and Trevor McCalla .

Billy Sullivan's Bugatti. Photo Bugatti Trust.

14. D Taylor, Bugatti Type 37 GP, 1,496 cc.

Captain Derrick Taylor (London) apparently had plenty of experience driving at Brooklands but had not taken part in any road races in Ireland before,

The car was described as a full Grand Prix four cylinder Bugatti.

15. E Griffiths Hughes, Frazer Nash TT Replica, 1,496 cc.

Not much was recorded about this driver other than he was from Cambridge, England. The car was a TT Replica model and *"as enthusiasts know, possesses a terrific performance. While the driver has raced at Brooklands, this will be his first road race in Ireland."* (UAC Monthly Review)

He gets a mention in the book Brooklands to Goodwood (Rodney Walkerley) - at the 1935 members meeting races at Donnington Park he won the Three Lap Handicap III in a Frazer Nash.

16. K N Hutchinson, Ford V8, 3,622 cc.

Kenneth Noel (Nonnie) Hutchinson (London, born 1910) competed in a wide range of different cars, including a chain drive Frazer Nash and a Type 37 Bugatti. In 1933 he set a new lap record at Donington Park in the Bugatti and he was also a successful trials driver.

"This apparently is a normal V8 Ford with various modifications and the driver is a well known Donington Park expert, having held the lap record on numerous occasions on a Bugatti." (UAC Monthly Review)

17. J Chambers, Riley, 1,089 cc.

William John (Jack) Chambers (Belfast, born 1915) was a well known local motor cycle racer (including sidecars). He won the Temple Motor Cycle Race as well as riding in many of the Ulster Grand Prix and North West 200 races.

The Riley was originally owned by W R (Bobby) Baird and was the car he drove in the 1933 Tourist Trophy race - coming 6th overall and 3rd in class.

The 1935 County Down Trophy was Jack Chamber's first road race.

18. J Wesley Shaw, Triumph, 1,232 cc s/c.

Following in his father James' footsteps, Wesley Shaw (Belfast, born 1914) raced both motorcycles and cars.

He started motorcycle racing in 1932 and competed at road races such as the Temple 100, Ulster Grand Prix and the Enniskillen 100 although without much success.

In 1934 he moved on to four wheel events, in particular reliability trials and rallying, reportedly winning every major reliability trial including the UAC Circuit of Ireland - always driving a Triumph car (his family were the Northern Ireland dealers).

According to the UAC the Triumph entered for the County Down Trophy was based on a Southern Cross chassis with a supercharger added. In an article on the website vintagenorton.com it says the car was specially built by Triumph and sent over for the County Down Trophy Race.

19. W F Ayrton, MG N Type Magnette, 1,287 cc.

"This car is a direct descendant of the type of car that won last year's TT, and although with an ordinary touring body, it should be capable of high speeds." (UAC Monthly Review).

Belfast man Ayrton, driving a 1,250 cc MG, came third in the first County Down Trophy Race in 1934. He was a UAC committee member and regular competitor in many local motor sport events. In March 1935 he went into business with a Mr W A T Hunter to establish Hunter & Ayrton (Belfast) Ltd, 47 May Street, Belfast, authorised agents for Armstrong Siddeley and MG cars.

21. W A Bartlett, C&T Special, 1,497 cc.

I have not been able to find out anything about W A Bartlett other than he was from Belfast.

Conquor & Topping entered the C&T special - a *"composite car having a Meadows engine"* according to the UAC.

It was a Northern Ireland company and that is all I know about it. There is a photo of the car on page 149.

22. H W Furey, MG N Type Magnette, 1,287 cc.

H W (Walter) Furey (Bangor, born 20 October 1913) came from an old Bangor family with extensive business interests in the area. This included a shop on Main Street which was one of the streets that made up the Bangor course.

There was a member of the Bangor Motor Sport Committee named W Furey but if this is Walter the racing driver or another member of the family I do not know.

According to Motor Sport magazine (October 1936) the car started life as a RN type saloon.

The UAC commented that *"the driver is a Bangor resident so he is certain to know the course better than most people."*

Walter Furey in his MG Magnette.
Photo with thanks to the British Newspaper Archive.

Derrick Taylor, Bugatti, passing the Hugh Furey Ltd shop on Bangor Main St. Photo North Down Museum website.

23. John R Hodge, MG N Type Magnette, 1,287 cc.

John Hodge (London) competed in the June 1934 County Down Trophy Race at Donaghadee coming 6th in his white streamlined Singer Le Mans. He was described as driving *"with verve"* although he became more cautious after going into a hedge at McCoubrey's corner.

A couple of weeks after Donaghadee, again in the Singer, he was part of the Junior Racing Drivers team at the British Automobile Racing Club (BARC) inter club meeting. The team came first and won the Stanley Cup.

**John Hodge and his MG Magnette in the pits.
Photo Johnson collection.**

24. A Carr, Lagonda Rapier De Clifford Special, 1,084 cc.

Archie Carr (Belfast) was a director of the local Lagonda agents Carr Gallagher Ltd. In an article by Peter Walby (UVCC Spring Bulletin 2018) it states that Carr Gallagher Ltd bought this car from Dobson & De Clifford Ltd, Staines, Middlesex in the spring of 1935.

The car may have been built specially to race at Le Mans (which could explain the De Clifford special designation) and did compete there in 1934, driven by Lord De Clifford (it came 16th). It was said to be extremely fast.

Archie Carr entered a Lagonda in the Ulster Motor rally earlier in 1935 but I do not know if it was the same car.

LAGONDA
ANNOUNCE
their comprehensive
1935 RANGE
OF MODELS AND PRICES

4¼ litre Rapide Chassis	...	...	£825
" " Tourer	...	...	£1000
4¼ litre standard Chassis	...	...	£675
" " Tourer	...	...	£825
" " Saloon	...	...	£950
3½ litre Chassis	...	...	£550
" Tourer	...	...	£695
" Saloon	...	...	£795
3 litre Chassis	...	...	£550
" Tourer	...	...	£695
" Saloon	...	...	£750
16.80 Chassis	...	...	£475
" Tourer	...	...	£595
" Family Saloon	...	...	£650
" Speed Saloon	...	...	£695
"Rapier" Chassis	...	...	£270

1935 Rapier Saloon and Tourer in Stock.
Demonstration Run can be Arranged.

SOLE DISTRIBUTORS FOR NORTHERN IRELAND:

CARR GALLAGHER LTD.
5, LITTLE KING STREET   -   BELFAST

25. L R Briggs, MG Midget, 847 cc.

Flight Lieutenant Llewelyn Rolls Briggs (born England 1897) moved to Greenisland, Northern Ireland in 1924 when he married into a local well-to-do Lawther family from Mount Vernon in Belfast.

He bought the MG J2 Midget in April 1933 and was soon competing in local motorsport events (including coming first in class at Craigantlet Hill Climb). Driving the same car he did extremely well at the first County Down Trophy Race at Donaghadee in 1934 until a big end bearing went in the engine after the 23rd lap.

The UAC Monthly Review described Briggs' entry as follows:

"This car will be remembered for its fine display in last year's race when it led for a considerable period before retiring with engine trouble. It is said to be even faster with a new streamlined body.

The driver is one of the best type, and while indulging in no fireworks, gets his car around corners quicker than most."

26. F H ffrench Davis, FIAT Balilla, 995 cc.

I have not been able to uncover any significant information about Francis H ffrench Davis. He was from the Dublin but the car was entered by Dick & Co, the Belfast FIAT dealer.

His reserve driver was J F Sutherland.

"This is one of the Balilla Fiats which are very popular in Italy on account of their good performance, and it is interesting to note that one of these cars completed 1,000 miles in the mountain circuit at Brooklands, at an average sped of 55 mph." UAC Monthly Review

Michael Sedgwick briefly mentions ffrench Davis in his book FIAT and credits the County Down Trophy Race as "an auspicious beginning for the small band of Irish Fiats which were to enjoy a long and distinguished career."

Dublin driver Francis H ffrench Davis.
Photo with thanks to the British Newspaper Archive.

28. R A Scott, MG, 847 cc.

This was Belfast motor salesman Robin Scott's first road race although he did compete in the 1934 Circuit of Ireland Trial in his MG. The car was described by the UAC as *"one of the usual MG Midgets with several interesting modifications"*.

Robin Scott at the start of the 1935 Ulster Motor Rally. Photo UAC Archive.

29. M H Fleming, MG, 847 cc.

M H (Malcolm) Fleming (born 1915) was from the Antrim Road area of Belfast and a former pupil of Belfast Royal Academy. A motor engineer, he was described in newspapers as not long out of his teens and the car as *"one of the ordinary MG's."*

He competed in the 1934 County Down Trophy Race at Donaghadee in the same car and came 10th, the last car to finish.

30. J McGrattan, MG, 847 cc.

Bangor man J McGrattan also competed in the 1934 Down Trophy Race in his MG. He came 7th, his average speed of 51.67 mph notably faster than Fleming (49.31 mph).

Bangor man J McGrattan in his MG. Photo with thanks to the British Newspaper Archive.

Officials and volunteers

A small army of officials and other volunteers was required for both the practice on the Thursday and the race itself. There are fifty-nine officials listed in the official programme including twenty-one doctors and eight timekeepers. This does not include the marshals and the police deployed around the course.

In addition there were 12 ambulance stations and 7 motor ambulances. The motor ambulances were on loan from:

Bangor Borough Council
Belfast Board of Guardians
Newtownards Board of Guardians
The Ulster Volunteer Force Hospital
Messrs. Melville & Co Ltd and
W M Wilton Esq

Details of the officials listed in the programme are included in Appendix 2.

The Handicap system

As in 1934 the handicap worked in terms of credit laps rather than time. One of the advantages of this approach was that it allowed a grid start.

The fastest (scratch) drivers had zero credit laps - they had to drive the full 25 laps to finish.

The slowest (limit) drivers had six credit laps - they only had to drive 19 laps to finish. In theory every car would finish in around 2 hours.

The number of laps each driver had to complete to finish (allowing for handicap credit laps) was as follows:

1935 Handicaps

Driver	Car	Laps to complete
1. L Fontés	Alfa Romeo s/c	25
2. A Dobson	Alfa Romeo s/c	25
4. W T McCalla	Sunbeam s/c	24
5. I F Connell	Vale s/c	24
6. S C Collier	MG Magnette	24
7. H C McFerran	Bugatti	24
9. L P Driscoll	Austin s/c	23
10. P Dwyer	Bugatti	23
11. C G Neill	Bugatti	23
12. W Sullivan	Bugatti	23
14. D Taylor	Bugatti	23
15. E Griffith Hughes	Frazer Nash	22
16. K N Hutchinson	Ford	22
17. J Chambers	Riley	22
18. J W Shaw	Triumph s/c	22
19. W F Ayrton	MG Magnette	21
21. W A Bartlett	C & T Special	21
22. H W Furey	MG Magnette	21
23. J Hodge	MG Magnette	21
24. A Carr	Lagonda	21
25. L R Briggs	MG Midget	20
26. F H ffrench Davis	FIAT Balilla	20
28. R A Scott	MG Midget	19
29. M H Fleming	MG Midget	19
30. J McGrattan	MG Midget	19

Race day - 22 June 1935

To finish first, first you have to finish and in 1935 only nine of the twenty five cars that started were classed as finishers.

The reports in the newspapers and magazines, understandably focus on the fastest cars and the eventual winners. Some of the drivers, especially in the middle of the grid, barely get a mention unless they crashed or the car broke down. I have tried to establish what happened to each of the twenty-five drivers but there are gaps.

One of the difficulties is, after lap one, not all the reports agree on what lap things happened. For example one reporter will say X happened after three laps, another will say it happened on the fourth lap or, if the driver had three credit laps, the reporter may say it happened after their sixth lap.

In the following pages the number of laps completed by each car when they retired comes from the race report printed in UAC Monthly Review August 1935.

The single seater Austin (9) in the pits prior to the race starting. Photo Dermot Johnson Snr.

The weather was by all accounts glorious - if anything too hot. At 2.30 pm A H Wilkinson in his Riley (registration CZ 6611) closed the roads.

At 3 pm the cars were being marshalled into position on the grid. Grid positions were determined by practice times (not handicap) and the drivers on the first three rows were:

First row: Luis Fontés (Alfa Romeo), Austin Dobson (Alfa Romeo) and Pat Driscoll (Austin)

Second row: W Sullivan (Bugatti) and I F Connell (Vale)

Third row: W T McCalla (Sunbeam), H C McFerran (Bugatti) and P Dwyer (Bugatti)

Cars being moved into position on the grid. Photo Dermot Johnson Snr.

Waiting for the race to start. Photo Dermot Johnson Snr.

As this was a handicap race the fastest car would not necessarily be the winner. The three cars on the front row had no credit laps - they had to complete 25 laps to finish. At the back of the grid the three MG Midgets had 6 credit laps

To win Fontés, Dobson or Driscoll had to be the first to complete 25 laps before, for example, Scott, Fleming or McGrattan completed 19 laps. It was a big ask but, if the handicapper's calculations were right, possible.

At ten past three the majority of engines had started and *"the noise rose to a crescendo as the Union Jack was raised, and when it fell every car leapt off its mark like a whippet."* (UAC Monthly Review) The Autocar described the start as spectacular.

And they're off - the massed start. Dobson was quickest away.
Photo UAC Archive.

Dobson in the number 2 Alfa Romeo made the slightly quicker start with Fontés very close behind and then Driscoll in the Austin. Last away was Taylor in the number 14 Bugatti. Within seconds there was dead silence in Abbey Street as all the cars headed towards Belfast on the first leg of the course and Clandeboye crossroads.

**From the start on Abbey Street onto the Belfast Road.
Photo with thanks to the British Newspaper Archive.**

It was not long before the spectators at the start/finish line in Abbey Street could hear the distinctive whine of the Alfa Romeo superchargers as they came down Gray's Hill. In a little under 4 1/2 minutes both Dobson and Fontés came past the pits almost abreast.

Connell in the Vale, having caught and passed Driscoll, was in third place.

Wesley Shaw (Triumph) hit the sandbags at Grey's Hill on the first lap but was able to continue.

Dobson and Fontés battle it out for the lead.
Photo Johnson collection.

Carr was the first to drop out, the Lagonda retiring on the first lap between Bangor West and Pickie[4] with ignition problems (a description which covers a multitude of possible causes).

On the second lap the two Alfa Romeo drivers remained neck and neck as they approached the start/finish - the radiator of the Fontés car level with Dobson's front wheel. The timekeepers could not divide them and both were credited with completing the lap in 4 minutes 25 seconds, an average of 80.75 mph and two seconds quicker than the first lap .

---

[4] The Pickie Pool - a well known Bangor Tourist attraction

Dobson leading Fontés into Main Street from Queen's Parade. Photo UAC Archive.

Collier (MG) moved into third place, Driscoll in the supercharged Austin was in fourth position and going well.

While the crowds were focussing on the thrilling battle between the two Alfa Romeo drivers, the race positions on the scoreboard, taking into account the number of credit laps each driver had, told a different story.

Although the Alfa Romeo drivers were the fastest cars at this point, they were not winning the race. The positions on handicap were R A Scott (MG Midget) with his six credit laps in first place followed by M H Fleming who also had six credit laps.

However the race had been going for less than 10 minutes - there was plenty of time for things to change.

Lap 2 saw local man Walter Furey retire. He went wide on the corner from Queen's Parade into Main Street and hit the sandbags. He was not hurt but the steering on the MG was damaged.

Some reports suggest that Furey continued after the crash and retired on lap 6. I think this is wrong as there is a photograph showing him, with the help of spectators and police, moving the car behind the sandbags. The confusion may have arisen because he had four handicap credit laps.

Walter Furey hits the sandbags at the bottom of Main St. Photo with thanks to the British Newspaper Archive.

When the two Alfa Romeo drivers appeared at the end of their third lap they were still together and flashed through the pits neck and neck - their lap speed again over 80 mph. Driscoll moved briefly into third place but soon had to call into the pits to have plugs changed and refuel.

Two further cars retired on the third lap - the Taylor Bugatti (thrown con rod) and the McGrattan MG.

On the fourth lap Fontés went in front but both his and Dobson's progress was slowed when they were flagged to slow down by marshals at Gray's Hill due to a dog loose on the course. This didn't prevent Fontés making what would turn out to be the fastest lap of the race - 82.87 mph - and passing the pits 10 seconds in front of Dobson.

The previous years winner, Trevor McCalla in the Sunbeam, despite starting on the third row of the grid, made little impact on the race and retired on the 4th lap with ignition problems, much to the disappointment of the crowd.

Trevor McCalla (4) in the Sunbeam just on front of Billy Sullivan (12) in the Bugatti. Photo UAC Archive.

On lap 5 Fontés was pushing the Alfa Romeo hard and increased his lead over Dobson to over 13 seconds. Coming along Queens's Parade from Gray's Hill he went broadside, much to the delight of the spectators. He quickly corrected the skid and tore up Main Street.

Driscoll in the supercharged Austin single seater was also providing fireworks and lapped the course in 4 minutes 47 seconds, a 30 second improvement on his handicap.

Driscoll was even faster on lap 6 with a remarkable time of 4 minutes 35 seconds (77.75 mph).

Pat Driscoll (9) in the Austin with Ian Connell (5) in the Vale behind. Photo Johnson collection.

Things were not going well for Gordon Neill and on lap six, hoping to sort out a bad engine misfire, he brought his Bugatti into the pits to change the plugs before rejoining the race. On the same lap Hugh McFerran also brought his Bugatti into the pits for a change of plugs.

Above: Hugh McFerran (7) Bugatti & W F Ayrton (19) MG. Below: Gordon Neill (11) Bugatti.
Photos Johnson collection.

At the end of the 7th lap Fontés was averaging 79.95 mph but the engine had developed a misfire. He brought the green Alfa Romeo into the pits and it was still being worked on when Dobson's crimson Alfa Romeo sped past for the second time. Then came the announcement that Fontés was retiring and the car, apparently with burnt out valves, was pushed off the course.

Dobson and Driscoll were now the two fastest drivers left in the race.

Five Bugatti drivers started the race and four were still going strong. Billy Sullivan, in Hugh McFerran's old Bugatti, was driving with almost unbelievable consistency - by the end of his 7th lap he had driven six successive laps at 4 min 45 secs (over 75 mph)!

Bugatti drivers Billy Sullivan (12) and Dwyer (10) at Crawfordsburn corner. Photo UAC Archive.

The other three Bugatti drivers, Dwyer, Neill and McFerran were still in the race.

Hugh McFerran, Bugatti, Bangor West railway bridge. Photo Bugatti Trust.

Wesley Shaw in the supercharged Triumph managed to avoid serious damage to the car when he hit sand bags at the top of Gray's Hill earlier in the race and overall was driving very consistently. However he was steadily losing ground to fellow motorcycle racer Jack Chambers in the Riley. Shaw was about a minute behind Chambers when, on his 8th lap, the supercharger on the Triumph broke and his race was over.

Driscoll, in the supercharged Austin single seater, put in a slow 10th lap, over 5 minutes. Bartlett, in the Conquor & Topping Special, retired on his 10th lap with gearbox and slipping clutch problems.

Ayrton in the MG Magnette retired with engine problems on his 11th lap. Driscoll put in another slow lap but with a handicap of two credit laps remained in front of Dobson on the scoreboard. On his 12th lap the car stopped part way round the course and it was eight minutes before he reappeared. However after that *"he got into his old stride."*

Bartlett (21), Conquor & Topping Special, retired on his 10th lap with gearbox and slipping clutch problems.
Photo Johnson collection.

While Dobson, Driscoll, Sullivan and others scorched around the course, they still had to overhaul the cars with more credit laps on handicap. If the handicapper's calculations were accurate this would not happen until the last few laps of the race.

At the end of thirteen laps the scoreboard showed the first three places were held by three MG drivers, Scott, Fleming and McGrattan, all with handicaps of six credit laps. In fourth place was ffrench Davis, FIAT, with 5 credit laps.

Scott had been driving particularly well and was almost four minutes in advance of the time the handicappers had expected him to achieve.

On his 15th lap Hugh McFerran in the number 7 Bugatti retired with magneto problems.

Driscoll's 16th lap was another very fast one, 4 minutes 35 seconds (77.5 mph) but Dobson in the Alfa Romeo was said to be 10 seconds faster. Despite Driscoll having a 2 credit lap advantage, Dobson was now in front of him.

Dwyer in the number 10 Bugatti retired in dramatic fashion on his 16th lap. In an effort to make up time he was taking the railway bridge at Bangor West ever faster. Like many cars going over the bridge he went airborne but this time when the car landed it ran onto the footpath, hit the sandbags and overturned. The car was badly damaged but Dwyer, thankfully with only minor abrasions and a dislocated thumb, was able to walk back to the pits. Only three Bugattis were now left in the race.

Scott was still in front on handicap (with 6 credit laps he only had to drive 19 to finish) but on his 17th lap the exhaust on the MG came loose. Braking severely to come into the pits, he spun the car around completely. He had a two and a half minute lead over Fleming but it took four minutes to get the car facing the right direction, tie up the exhaust with copper wire and get going again.

Shortly afterwards it was announced that Scott had retired as the engine had run a big end bearing.

Both Driscoll and Jack Chambers retired on their 18th lap. Driscoll came to a halt in a hollow part way around the course when the Austin developed ignition problems. The fault was traced to a defective switch wire but the car could not be restarted without being pushed and outside assistance would have meant disqualification.

Driscoll's best lap was 4 minutes 42 seconds, representing 75.82 mph. His speed through the pits was estimated to be over 100 mph.

Jack Chambers had worked his way up to 5th place before retiring. According to most reports the Riley blew a head gasket. However one report added that there was also a hole in the sump!

28 Robin Scott (MG) followed by 26 ffrench Davis (FIAT). Dobson in the number 2 Alfa Romeo at the back is waiting for a chance to pass. Photo with thanks to Simon Thomas.

Gordon Neill in the number 11 Bugatti had no end of misfortune. In addition to the engine starting to misfire early in the race, he also burst a tyre when he hit sandbags at the top of Gray's Hill and had to limp back to the pits to get it changed.

The engine misfire problem frequently returned but Gordon battled on until his 19th lap before finally retiring.

Only ten cars were now left in the race. Malcolm Fleming moved from second into first place when Scott retired and, providing he did not mess up and the MG stuck the pace, would be hard to beat.

At the beginning of the 23rd lap Fleming was still in first place, ffrench Davis was second, Briggs third and Collier fourth. Davis spun completely around in Main Street but according to the Northern Whig he *"righted himself quickly and was off like a hare"* without losing position.

Fully aware that there were only three laps remaining Sullivan and Dobson stepped up the pace. On the last laps Sullivan moved up to third place and Dobson to fifth place and they were still in these positions when the race ended.

Malcolm Fleming in the number 29 MG took the chequered flag followed by ffrench Davis and Sullivan. Six other drivers finished.

K N Hutchinson in the number 16 Ford ran out of time. He had completed 24 laps (including his 3 credit laps) when the race was declared over and he was flagged off.

Opposite page:

Top right: Malcolm Fleming takes the chequered flag.
Photo with thanks to the British Newspaper Archive.
Bottom right: The winner with family and friends.
Photo author's collection.

The 1935 Results

Result	Driver and race number	Car	Average MPH
1st	M H Fleming (29)	MG, 847 cc	61.83
2nd	F H ffrench Davis (26)	FIAT, 995 cc	64.48
3rd	W Sullivan (12)	Bugatti, 1990 cc	73.97
4th	L R Briggs (25)	MG, 847 cc	63.69
5th	A Dobson (2)	Alfa Romeo, 2600 cc	78.76
6th	S C Collier (6)	MG, 1087 cc s/c	73.55
7th	E Griffiths-Hughes (15)	Frazer Nash, 1496 cc	57.51
8th	I F Connell (5)	Vale, 1496 cc s/c	71.70
9th	J Hodge (23)	MG, 1287 cc	62.74

Fastest lap: L Fontés, Alfa Romeo, 2336 cc s/c
4 minutes 18 seconds, average speed 82.87 mph

Team Prize
Team B: I F Connell (Vale), E Griffiths-Hughes (Frazer Nash) and J Hodge (MG Magnette).

Opposite page:
Above: ffrench Davis came 2nd in the FIAT Balilla.
Below: Sam Collier from New York came 6th in the MG Magnette.

Flight Lieutenant L R Briggs (25) in the MG Midget came 4th. J Chambers in the number 17 Riley retired on his 18th lap.

Opposite page

Top: E Griffiths Hughes, Frazer Nash (15), finished in 7th place.

Bottom: Ian Connell (5) in the supercharged Vale Special finished in 8th place despite hitting a dog early in the race.

All photos Johnson collection.

**John Hodge (23) in the MG Magnette finished in 9th place.
Photo Johnson collection.**

K N Hutchinson, Ford, had not completed 25 laps (including handicap credits) by the time the race was declared over. Photo Johnson collection.

After the race

There was a huge crowd at the prize giving in Caproni's Palais de Danse. The prizes were distributed by the Lady Mayoress and, although they did not finish in the top four, both Austin Dobson and Sam Collier received souvenir awards.

The UAC Monthly Review published an article by R H Wright, senior timekeeper at both motorcycle and motor car races in Northern Ireland, with the title *The County Down Trophy Race in Retrospect*. The following is from the opening paragraphs:

"Whatever may be the future of the race for the County Down Trophy there can be no doubt that the 1935 event at Bangor was a success in every aspect, except perhaps one, and that one - the unreliability of cars entered - completely outside the control of the Club.

The attendance of spectators was outside anything experienced at Club events before. Wave after wave of passengers billowed from the railway station to spread over the town in search of vantage points - cars, buses, bicycles and pedestrians converged on the course from every point on the compass, and Bangor must have had an influx rarely experienced in its history. This indicated widespread interest in the event, and showed clearly how this interest was enhanced by the convenience of access to the course.

The entry, both in quality and quantity, was all that could be desired, ranging from the speedy Alfa Romeos on the scratch mark to the more modest "baby" cars at the limit. Of particular interest was the Austin which, though having the smallest engine in the race, was, in fact one of the fastest cars in the event"

All the papers agreed on one thing - the event was both a success and better than the year before.

The 1936 International County Down Trophy Race

Bangor - motor sport capital of Ulster

I have always taken it for granted that the 1936 International County Down Trophy Race would be held in Bangor on the same circuit used in 1935. The success of the 1935 event was due, in no small part, to the support the town council provided and the work of the Bangor Motor Sports Committee. In addition the UAC Circuit of Ireland Trial was going to start and finish in Bangor that year.

Surely there was never any possibility that it would not go ahead or be held anywhere other than Bangor? It was already in the international motorsport calendar.

Life is seldom that straightforward. At a Bangor Council meeting towards the end of January 1936 there was a discussion on whether or not a race should be held in Bangor that year.

Councillor McMillan, concerned about the impact of closing the main roads on traders, wanted *"an open country race" - only pubs and tobacconists benefited from the race"* in 1935.

Councillor Milligan was concerned about *"the promotion of speed rather than moderation, speed being an incentive to the young bloods of the town."*

A motion was passed (by 10 votes to 2) instructing the Town Clerk *"to ascertain from 1,000 rate payers their views as to whether a race should be held or not"*. It seems the exercise did not go ahead as in July the same councillor again called for a survey of ratepayers opinions regarding the race.

There was another protest about the Down Trophy Race, this time on behalf of the Automobile Club de l'Ouest (ACO) in France, the Le Mans 24 hour race organisers.

There was considerable political turmoil in France that year and a late change to the date of Le Mans race meant it clashed with the Down Trophy Race.

The RAC duly protested to the international motor sport governing body but few expected them to choose a small road race in Northern Ireland over the famous Le Mans 24 hour.

To the surprise of many the decision was in favour of the International County Down Trophy Race and the French changed the date of the Le Mans race to one in August. However continuing trade union and other protests in France resulted in Le Mans not running at all that year.

In February 1936 Bangor Council received approval from the Minister for Home Affairs to spend *"a sum not exceeding £50 as first prize in connection with the annual Motor Rally to finish in Bangor and also a sum not exceeding £50 as a guarantee to the joint committee which would be responsible for running the Co. Down Trophy Road race on Saturday 20th June."*

Bangor was, in 1936, the motor sport capital of Ulster!

Changes for 1936

There were actually very few changes for 1936. The UAC were told at the start of the year of plans to build a roundabout at the junction of the Conlig-Belfast roads, just after Abbey Street. The Club felt this chicane would not *"detract in the slightest either from the speed or the interest in the race."* In the end the roundabout was not built until after the race so the course remained much as it was in 1935.

At least some competitors wanted the distance of the race to be increased (more laps) but the Club, conscious of complaints about the impact on traders, decided to leave the distance of the race unchanged at 150 miles.

The regulations were also the same as in 1935 but the entry fee was increased from three guineas to four guineas which the UAC argued was more than reasonable:

"For four guineas the racing motorist gets a 150 miles road race with a chance of winning £100, whereas elsewhere he will be having to pay double or treble to get even less value. The only extra is the compulsory third party premium of £2, which brings the entry fee up to the very modest sum of £6 4s 0d."

I have not found any records or reports suggesting that starting money was paid for any County Down Trophy Race.

Nothing succeeds like success and the 1935 event was certainly a success. The Prime Minister of Northern Ireland, Viscount Craigavon, decided to attend the 1936 race and if you look at the list of officials in Appendix 2 you will see that Viscount Castlereagh was now one of the Stewards of the meeting.

The main prizes were similar to 1935 with a few additions. William Noble generously provided a cup for the fastest time and Fred Rogers a trophy for the fastest lap.

In addition, all drivers completing the race within the allotted time who did not win prizes would receive a solid silver ashtray courtesy of F M Heyn.

The Awards

1st prize - The County Down Trophy (to be held for one year) plus replica and the sum of £50, presented by the townspeople of Bangor.

2nd Prize: A replica of the trophy and the sum of £50, presented by the licensed traders of Bangor.

3rd prize: A replica of the trophy and £35 presented by Mr E Caproni.

4th prize: A replica of the trophy plus £10, presented by the motor traders of Bangor.

Team prize: £15 15 s 0d (15 guineas), presented by the motor traders of Bangor.

Prize for the fastest time of the race: a cup presented by W Noble.

Prize for the fastest lap: a trophy presented by F H Rogers.

Souvenir for drivers completing the race but who did not win awards presented by F M Heyn.

The 1936 Entrants

The number of entries was capped (by the RAC) at forty and thirty-six entries were received by the closing date compared to thirty the year before. A list of all the entrants and drivers is included in Appendix 3. Fifteen of the entries were from England, five from the Irish Free State and the rest were local drivers.

The breakdown of marques entered is interesting. Half the cars entered were either MG (11) or Bugatti (7).

The entries which caused the most excitement for motor racing enthusiasts were the three, new for 1936, overhead camshaft supercharged Austin 744 cc single seat cars, the two ERAs and the ALTA (entered by A A Millard).

The return of the Fontés' Alfa Romeo, this time driven by Englishman Anthony Powys-Lybbe, also caused much excitement. Although the car retired at the previous years County Down Trophy Race it remained *"perhaps the most illustrious car in the British Isles at the present moment"* with an impressive list of victories.

What most excited the Press was the person entering a new eight cylinder supercharged "golden" Bugatti and its driver. The entrant was an exiled Georgian Princess[5], Nina Mdivani, and the driver was Adrian, youngest son of Sir Arthur Conan Doyle. His brother Denis (who was engaged to the Princess) was the reserve driver.

If getting the Princess to enter the car was a publicity stunt (Adrian Conan Doyle could easily have entered it himself), it worked brilliantly. News of the entry made headlines across the papers and photographers were keen to spot the Princess and her entourage whenever they appeared in Bangor.

---

[5] The legitimacy of the title has been much debated.

Apparently her presence even overshadowed that of Lord Craigavon, the Prime Minister of Northern Ireland.

For weeks after the race interviews with the Princess appeared in the society columns of the local papers.

Denis Conan Doyle standing beside fiancée Princess Nina Mdivani and her Golden Bugatti in the pits at Bangor. Photo with thanks to the British Newspaper Archive.

Race Practice - 18 June 1936

Scrutineering was, as in previous years, in the J B Ferguson garage in Chichester Street Belfast on the day before practice (Wednesday 17).

On their way from Dublin to scrutineering J Tookey and R Cavangah (I think in the Ford entered by Smithfield Motors Ltd) were involved in an accident at Banbridge.

According to the North Down Herald their car struck a kerb and they were thrown out of the car onto the road. All four wheels on the car were ripped off. They were taken to Banbridge District Hospital suffering from severe head and back injuries.

The timekeepers had already decided on the handicaps for each car but the position on the grid also depended on how fast the driver was in practice. In addition all drivers (including reserves) had to complete three laps in practice above a minimum speed set by the timekeepers.

Large crowds turned out for the practice. The UAC had suggested that spectators might want to bring stopwatches so they could work out for themselves how fast the cars were going. The programme helpfully included a table converting lap time into speed.

There were a few minor dramas during practice. Trevor McCalla and A R Finlay managed somehow to collide just after the start. Thankfully both drivers were uninjured and there was no serious damage to the cars. J P Almack crashed his Riley near Clandeboye and buckled a wheel. Jackie Chambers generously collected a spare wheel from pits and brought it to the stricken Riley. Chambers, in a further act of generosity, also lent the Almack reserve driver, J Hutton Harrop, a car so he could qualify.

Charlie Manders was racing in the motorcycle TT on the Isle of Man earlier that day. Immediately after his race, as pre-arranged, he boarded a light aircraft and flew to Newtownards airfield where a car was waiting for him. With the permission of the Stewards, the Adler was sitting at Clandeboye corner and he was able to complete his qualifying laps. He then returned to Newtownards airfield and flew back to the Isle of Man.

Charlie Manders (28), Adler, coming from Bangor West. Photo Johnson collection.

J P Almack (Riley), J Bell (Conquer & Topping Special) and F Cassidy (MG entered by L Liddel) failed to qualify.

The fastest lap times and speeds set at practice are below:

1936 Practice lap times and speed

Driver	Car	Lap time	Speed (mph)
Powys-Lybbe	Alfa Romeo s/c	4 min 13 secs	84. 51
P N Whitehead	ERA s/c	4 min 14 secs	84.18
C J P Dodson	Austin s/c	4 min 36 secs	74 .77
L P Driscoll	Austin s/c	4 min 36 secs	74 .77
G F A Manby-Colegrave	ERA s/c	4 min 37 secs	81.18
W R Baird	MG s/c	4 min 46 secs	74.76
Derrick Taylor	Bugatti s/c	4 min 47 secs	74.50
Duke of Grafton	Squire s/c	4 min 49 secs	73.98
C L Goodacre	Austin s/c	4 min 54 secs	72.72
Ivo Peters	Frazer Nash	4 min 54 secs	72.72
Adrian Conan-Doyle	Bugatti s/c	4 min 54 secs	72.72
F H ffrench Davis	FIAT	4 min 58 secs	71.73
A A Millard	ALTA s/c	4 min 59 secs	71.51
W Sullivan	FIAT	4 min 59 secs	71.51

L R Briggs (MG s/c) did one lap in 5 minutes (71.27 mph). The next fastest was the golden Bugatti reserve driver Denis Conan Doyle with a lap time of 5 minutes 3 seconds. Jackie Chambers (Riley) managed one lap in 5 minutes and 5 seconds.

Trevor McCalla (Sullivan Special s/c) and Walter Furey (MG) were slower than expected.

The best lap time for both C G Neil (Bugatti) and A R Finlay (MG) was 5 minute 17 seconds. According to the report in the North Down Herald the "small cars, as a rule, were not far off the time set by the handicapper for the race."

By contrast the fastest lap Powys-Lybbe set in practice (4 min 13 secs) was 24 secs faster than the handicappers calculations (4 min 37 seconds). Both he and G F A Manby-Colegrave were scratch - they had to drive 25 laps to finish.

Bangor West railway bridge. Adrian Conan Doyle (9), Bugatti, in front followed by A P McArthur (24), MG. Photo Johnson collection.

Race day - 20 June 1936

Yet again the weather gods smiled on Bangor - the temperature was almost tropical. The course was in excellent condition. Clandeboye corner had been improved and all the roads had a recently applied anti slip surface, paid for by the local authorities.

The roads were closed at 2.30 pm by A H Wilkinson (now UAC vice chairman) with the Chief Marshal, Alderman W J Chambers in the passenger seat of the Riley.

AH Wilkinson driving, Chief Marshal W J Chambers is in the passenger seat. Photo UAC Archive.

Thirty-six cars entered the 1936 race and 32 were expected to start. Mervyn White (Bugatti) withdrew due to a hand injury and, as previously mentioned, one car was badly damaged in a crash near Banbridge. Two drivers, F Cassidy (MG) and J Bell (C & T Special) failed to qualify.

In fact only 31[6] drivers started. During practice the ex-Dick Seaman ERA driven by Peter Whitehead had set the second fastest lap before developing gearbox problems. The month before gearbox problems had caused Whitehead to retire on the starting line at the International Trophy Race at Brooklands.

A spare gearbox was rushed over from England on the morning of the race but was found to have the same fault and neither gearbox could be fixed in time.

1935 County Down Trophy winner Malcolm Fleming surrounded by admirers. Photo author's collection.

---

[6] Motor Sport & Autocar say there were 30 starters.

The 1936 Drivers

1. Anthony Powys-Lybbe, Alfa Romeo, 2,336 cc s/c.

Handicap: Scratch (0 credit laps) - 25 laps to finish.

Powys-Lybbe, Bradfield England, was no stranger to Ulster as he previously competed in the TT driving *"an old Alvis at terrific speed on the corners in an endeavour to make up for the all-out speed he lacked."* The Alfa Romeo was *"certainly the most remarkable car in the race and its past history should go a long way towards making it favourite."* (UAC Monthly Review)

This would be the second time this particular Alfa Romeo competed at Bangor. In 1935, driven by Luis Fontés, it set the fastest lap at 4 minutes 18 seconds (82.87 mph). The car retired after 7 laps with burnt out valves.

In 1936 Powys-Lybbe set the fastest lap in practice - 4 minutes,13 seconds (84.51 mph) and was on the front row of the grid.

Powys-Lybbe during practice. Photo Johnson Collection.

3. G F A Manby-Colegrave, ERA, 1,488 cc s/c.

Handicap: Scratch (0 credit laps) - 25 laps to finish.

G F A Manby-Colegrave, London, entered an MG Magna for the 1935 Down Trophy race but it was withdrawn without attending practice. He was a very experienced driver and had raced before in Ireland, for example at Phoenix Park and Bray.

The car (ERA R1B) was described by the UAC as *"one of the cars of the type that swept all before it in the 1 1/2 litre races, both in Great Britain and the Continent."* A similar ERA won the Cork road race in May 1936.

ERA R1B arrives at Bangor for practice.
Photo Johnson collection.

5. Derrick Taylor, Bugatti Type 51 GP, 2,263 cc s/c.

Handicap: 1 credit lap - 24 laps to finish.

Captain Taylor, London, competed in the 1935 Down Trophy race in a 1,496 cc Bugatti car but retired on the first lap with engine troubles. The experience obviously did not put him off as he returned for another go in a Type 51 Grand Prix Bugatti.

The 1936 car previously belonged to R O Shuttleworth and was capable of over 130 mph. It was, according to the UAC, capable of showing a clean pair of heels to most.

6. Charles Goodacre, Austin, 744 cc s/c.

Handicap: 1 credit lap - 24 laps to finish.

The new 744cc supercharged overhead camshaft Austins made their debut at the International Trophy Race at Brooklands earlier in 1936 but suffered from various mechanical issues and only one finished the race.

Charles (Charlie) Lindsey Goodacre, born West Kirby England 1909, was a successful racing driver but this was his first year competing at Bangor. In practice he was the slowest of the three Austin works drivers, with a fastest lap of 4 minutes 54 seconds (72.72 mph).

7. Charles Dodson, Austin 744 cc s/c.

Handicap: 1 credit lap - 24 laps to finish.

Charles Joseph Person Dodson, born Didsbury, England 1901. Well known as both a motor car and motorcycle racer, this was Dodson's first time at Bangor. He set the joint fastest lap time of the Austin works drivers at practice - 4 minutes 36 seconds (74.77 mph).

8. L P Driscoll, Austin, 744 cc s/c.

Handicap: 1 credit lap - 24 laps to finish.

Pat Driscoll competed in the 1935 Down Trophy in the older side valve Austin single seater. He set some incredibly fast laps before the car retired with ignition problems.

In practice in 1936 his fastest lap time was 4 minutes 36 seconds (74.77 mph), the same as Charles Dodson.

**The Charles Dodson Austin 744 cc supercharged racer.
Photo Johnson collection.**

9. Adrian Conan Doyle, Bugatti Type 51A, 1,492 cc s/c.

Handicap: 1 credit lap - 24 laps to finish.

The youngest son of the famous author Sir Arthur Conan Doyle, Adrian, according to the UAC, had no previous experience of road racing but had competed in the Southport sand races *"where he has had consistent success driving a big supercharged Mercedes."*

The Type 51A twin camshaft Grand Prix Bugatti was regarded as one of the most interesting cars in the race and was *"said to be one of the factories latest productions and is an 8-cylinder."*

The Adrian Conan Doyle Golden Bugatti.
Photo Johnson collection.

10. C G Neill, Bugatti Type 35 GP, 1,990 cc.

Handicap: 2 credit laps - 23 laps to finish.

Gordon Neill was a very well known local competitor and had been using this 1926 Type 35 Grand Prix Bugatti for the past two racing seasons. His best result was 3rd place in the Leinster Trophy race in 1935.

This was the third time he had entered the County Down Trophy Race. In 1934 he had to withdraw as he had not recovered from a crash at the Bray races a few weeks before. In 1935 his car retired on the 19th lap.

He may have been hoping that it would be third time lucky.

11. Duke of Grafton, Squire, 1,496 cc s/c.

Handicap: 2 credit laps - 23 laps to finish.

John Charles William Fitzroy, 9th Duke of Grafton, born 1st August 1914, was an inexperienced racing driver and had not competed at Bangor before. He was due to drive the Squire at the Cork races earlier in 1936 but he could not start the car on the day of the race.

The Squire was considered a very fine example of the modern supercharged sports car with guaranteed speed over 100 mph. Grafton's car was the second produced by the company and at practice set the eighth fastest lap time - 4 minutes 47 seconds (73.98 mph).

12. L R Briggs, MG K3, 1,087 cc s/c.

Handicap: 2 credit laps - 23 laps to finish.

Flight Lieutenant Briggs, originally from England but now living in Greenisland, County Antrim, was one of the best known and liked drivers in Northern Ireland - he was also described in the UAC Monthly Review Social Round column (by our woman correspondent) as *"the most handsome driver in the race."* The same correspondent described Powys-Lybbe as *"easily the most untidily dressed."*

Llewellyn Briggs consistent and fast driving style stood him in good stead in the previous County Down Trophy Races. In 1934, driving an 847 cc MG, he was leading when on the 24th lap the car retired after losing oil pressure. In 1935, in the same car, he came fourth. In addition to the County Down Trophy Races, Briggs also raced in the south of Ireland and on the Isle of Man.

The 1,087 cc supercharged MG K3 was the same model that Nuvolari drove to victory in the 1933 TT and, according to the UAC Monthly Review, *"the one in which Pellegrini put up such a fine show" in the Mille Miglia last year and can be regarded as one of the fastest cars in the North of Ireland. It has exceptional acceleration and superlative road-holding."*

Briggs had driven this car in the races at Cork and the Isle of Man the month before without much success and his performance during practice was barely noteworthy - he set the fifteenth fastest lap time - 5 minutes and no seconds (71.27 mph).

14. H C McFerran, Bugatti Type 35A GP, 1,990 cc.

Handicap: 2 credit laps - 23 laps to finish.

Hugh McFerran was another well known local driver. He competed in both the 1934 and 1935 County Down Trophy Races but on both occasions his Bugatti retired with mechanical problems. To add insult to injury in the 1935 race he was beaten by Billy Sullivan in a Bugatti he bought from McFerran.

1936 did not look like being any better as mechanical problems saw him retiring from his last four races.

For this years race, in addition to whatever mechanical work was carried out, the car was painted *"a resplendent shade of blue.'* The new colour does not appear to have brought an immediate change of fortune as the engine seized during practice. McFerran was able to qualify in a borrowed car and the engine was rebuilt on the Friday in a garage in Alfred Steet Belfast.

15. A A Millard, Alta, 1,074 cc s/c.

Handicap: 2 credit laps - 23 laps to finish.

Millard competed in a varsities race in 1935 driving a 1,496 cc Frazer Nash and this was his first time racing in Ireland. In practice his fastest lap was four minutes and 59 seconds (71.51 mph).

Founded in 1931 by Geoffrey Taylor the Alta Car & Engineering Company produced about twelve 1,074 cc supercharged sports cars. (British Racing Green, David Venables) The engine, designed by Taylor, had an aluminium block and shaft driven double overhead camshafts.

The cars were reputed to be good for 100 mph.

16. W R Baird, MG R type, 750 cc s/c.

Handicap: 2 credit laps - 23 laps to finish.

Bobby Baird was the one of the most experienced racing drivers in Northern Ireland at that time. He came 6th in the 1933 TT, and 13th in the 1935 TT. He also won several class awards in various Irish races.

Bobby entered both previous County Down Trophy Races. In 1934, on the 18th lap when it looked like he might win the race, the engine in his Riley blew up. In 1935 he qualified but was unable to compete when his mechanic was involved in a crash while driving the car the day before the race.

This year he was well up with the leaders in practice - his fastest lap was 4 minutes and 46 seconds (74.76 mph), significantly quicker than his handicap time (5 minutes and 1 second).

Bobby Baird, MG R type. Photo Johnson collection.

21. W Sullivan, FIAT, 995 cc.

Handicap: 3 credit laps - 22 laps to finish.

Popular local driver Billy Sullivan ran the Belfast Car Laundry Ltd garage in Victoria Square Belfast (where the Victoria Square shopping centre is now).

He came 5th in the first County Down Trophy Race at Donaghadee driving a 739 cc supercharged Sullivan Special - basically a highly tuned Morris. In the 1935 race he came 3rd after a brilliant drive in an ex-Hugh McFerran Bugatti. In 1936 his best lap time in practice was 4 minutes and 59 seconds (71.51 mph).

The Billy Sullivan FIAT. Photo Johnson collection.

18. Ivo Peters, Frazer Nash TT Replica, 1,496 cc.

Handicap: 3 credit laps - 22 laps to finish.

Ivo Peters from Bristol, England, came 5th in the Cork motor races on 16 May 1936 driving the Frazer Nash TT Replica.

The first Frazer Nash with the TT Replica designation was registered in March 1932 and in the TT races later that year a Frazer Nash driven by H J Aldington came 9th overall and first in class 6. Frazer Nash cars also took the top 4 places in class 6 in the 1934 TT races.

The UAC, possibly harshly, described the Frazer Nash as *"of a type which has run consistently without success in the Tourist Trophy, and is perhaps better known as a successful trials car."*

19. J Chambers, Riley 1,089 cc.

Handicap: 3 credit laps. 22 laps needed to finish.

Belfast man Jackie Chambers was best known as a motor cycle racer and held the lap record for several of the local motorcycle courses.

His Riley was driven by Bobby Baird in the 1933 TT when he came 6th overall. Chambers first motor race was the 1935 Down Trophy race and he put up a very creditable performance, working his way up to 5th place before the engine blew a head gasket and/or a hole in the sump depending on which report you read.

17. J R Morley, Bugatti,1,496 cc.

Handicap: 3 credit laps - 22 laps to finish.

The UAC had little to say about J R Morley other than he was new to Irish Races and the car he entered.

According to the UAC the Bugatti was identical to the one driven by Captain Derrick Taylor in the 1935 County Down Trophy Race which, if correct, would mean it was a Type 37.

J R Morley, Bugatti, in the pit area.
Photo Johnson collection.

20. J Hutton Harrop, Riley, 1,089 cc.

Handicap: 3 credit laps- 22 laps to finish.

The Riley was entered by The Almack Engineering Service with J P Almack as the driver and J Hutton Harrop as the reserve driver.

J P Almack buckled the wheel of the Riley when he crashed near Clandeboye during practice. Jackie Chambers brought a spare from the pits to get the car going again but the damage may have been more than just a buckled wheel as J P Almack failed to qualify. Hutton Harrop qualified driving a car borrowed from Jackie Chambers.

The Almack Riley was repaired in time for Hutton Harrop to drive it in the race.

22. A Hutchinson, MG, 939 cc s/c.

Handicap: 4 credit laps - 21 laps to finish.

I think, but cannot be certain, that this is the car entered by J W Patterson and Hutchinson is the *"young Ulsterman"* who did not want his identity to be known when the entry was submitted. The UAC described the car as *"one of the standard PB MG's with a low pressure blower fitted."*

Alan Hutchinson, from Castledawson, bought an MG PB (registration EZ 2444) in 1935 with a Marshall 75 supercharger, aero screen, bonnet strap and a rear axle ratio suited for racing.

He did not race in the two previous County Down Trophy Races and he is not listed as one of the drivers in the Bray races in 1934 or 1935. It is possible that the 1936 County Down Trophy was his first road race.

24. A P McArthur, MG Magnette, 1287 cc.

Handicap: 4 credit laps - 21 laps to finish.

I have seen this surname spelt three different ways (Macarthur, MacArthur and McArthur) but whichever is correct I know little about A P other than, according to Motor Sport, he was from the Irish Free State.

I assume he had competed in the Circuit of Ireland as the UAC described the car as a *"well-tuned Magnette, and most rally competitors will remember it for its wonderful exhaust note."*

The UAC was expecting Ernie Robb (son of a Dundonald garage owner) to drive the car but I am fairly certain he did not. There is no mention of Robb at practice and photographs of the car taken at the race name McArthur as the driver.

25. H W Furey, MG Magnette, 1,287 cc.

Handicap: 4 credit laps - 21 laps to finish.

Bangor man Walter Furey competed in the 1935 County Down Trophy Race where he gained *"perhaps the unenviable distinction of being one of the fastest over Bangor West railway bridge."*

He went out of the 1935 race quite early after he hit sandbags at the corner going into Main Street.

Furey, driving this MG, won the 200 mile race in Phoenix Park, Dublin, 14 September 1935 (average speed 69.91 mph).

26. A R Finlay, MG, 1,087 cc.

Handicap: 4 credit laps - 21 laps to finish.

Bangor man A R Finlay came second in the first County Down Trophy Race at Donaghadee in 1934. He had a bad crash at Phoenix Park later that year and it took a long time for him to recover from his injuries.

He did not compete in the 1935 race but, with driver and car now fully recovered, he was back in 1936 for another go.

27. F H ffrench Davis, FIAT, 995 cc.

Handicap: 4 credit laps - 21 laps to finish.

Dubliner ffrench Davis came second in the 1935 County Down Trophy Race as well as competing in the TT race (Class G) the same year (Hough, Tourist Trophy).

28. Charles Manders, Adler, 995 cc.

Handicap: 4 credit laps - 21 laps to finish.

This car was entered by Irischer Adler Renstall. Adler cars were assembled in the Irish Free State and the cars were very successful in a wide range of motor sport events, including the 1934 Bray Race and the Leinster Trophy Race.

Dublin born Charlie Manders was very well known in the 1930s mainly as a successful motorcycle rider and, as mentioned earlier, flew over from the Isle of Man TT races on Thursday 18 June so he could put in the necessary laps to qualify for the County Down Trophy Race.

 He was the agent for Sunbeam and other motorcycle makes as well as a director of the Leinster Motor Cycle and Light car Club.

30. W T McCalla, Sullivan Special, 849 cc s/c.

Handicap: 4 credit laps - 21 laps to finish.

Belfast born Trevor McCalla was a well known local competitor and won the first Down Trophy race driving the ex-Sir Henry Segrave 2 litre supercharged Sunbeam.

He drove the Sunbeam again in the 1935 Down Trophy race but retired on the 4th lap due to ignition problems.

The Sullivan Special was entered by Billy Sullivan with McCalla as the nominated driver.

Left: ffrench Davis in his FIAT Balilla. Photo Johnson collection.

31. J McGrattan, FIAT, 995 cc.

Handicap: 4 credit laps - 21 laps to finish.

I know relatively little about J McGrattan. He competed in the both previous County Down Trophy Races. In 1934 at Donaghadee he came 7th driving an 847 cc MG. He competed at Bangor in 1935, also in an MG, but was listed as a finisher.

The J McGrattan (31) FIAT. Number 30 behind is the Sullivan Special. Photo author's collection.

32. M H Fleming, MG, 847 cc.

Handicap: 5 credit laps - 20 laps to finish.

Malcolm Fleming came 10th in the first County Down Trophy Race at Donaghadee in 1934 and won the 1935 race at Bangor. Later the same year he came 4th in the Phoenix Park races in Dublin.

This was his third year competing in the County Down Trophy race in the same MG. *"What more can be said except that this driver will strain every nerve to retain the trophy he won last year."*(UAC Monthly Review)

The defending champion Malcolm Fleming in his MG.
Photo author's collection.

33. G A Mangan, MG P type, 847cc

Handicap: 5 credit laps, 20 laps to finish.

This car was entered by S R Sheane with George A Mangan as the nominated driver.

Mangan, according to Motor Sport magazine, was from the Irish Free State.

35. T J McCall, MG, 847 cc.

Handicap: 5 credit laps, 20 laps to finish.

The car was described as a standard P Type, the same model as driven by Malcolm Fleming.

T J McCall had no previous race experience as far as I know.

36. H B Prestwich, MG J3, 847 cc.

Handicap: 5 credit laps, 20 laps to finish.

H B Prestwich must have had some road racing experience as he competed in the 1934 Tourist Trophy race. He crashed at Quarry Corner badly damaging the car but, thankfully, only slightly injuring himself.

In the UAC Monthly Review the car is described as an MG J3 with the supercharger removed. It was reputed to be very fast.

37. H Weir, Ford Special, 993 cc.

Handicap: 5 credit laps, 20 laps to finish.

This car was entered by Belfast man Fred Smyth. The same car was entered for the 1935 Down Trophy but Smyth failed to qualify.

For 1936 Smyth opted to have H Weir drive. Weir did qualify at practice and, other than how he did in the race, that is all I know about him.

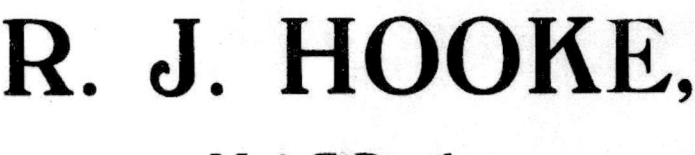

The 1936 Race

Cars getting into their positions for the massed start.
Photo North Down Museum.

At 3 pm the cars started to move into position on the grid, ready for the massed start. On the front row was Powys-Lybbe in the Alfa Romeo and Dodson in the works Austin. On the second row was G F A Manby-Colegrave in the ERA and Driscoll in another works Austin.

The Goodacre Austin proved difficult to start but eventually got going. At 3.15 pm Viscount Craigavon dropped the union flag and with a deafening roar the cars sped towards the bottle neck where Abbey Street met the Belfast Road.

Dodson in the supercharged Austin was quickest away followed by Manby-Colegrave in the ERA and then Powys -Lybbe in the Alfa Romeo. Within 2 miles the Alfa Romeo was at the front and when the cars reached the start/finish at the end of the first lap it was Powys-Lybbe at the front with Dodson 200 yards behind, then Driscoll, Manby-Colegrave and Conan Doyle.

On the second lap the fireworks started - Powys -Lybbe went round in 4 minutes 16 seconds (83.42 mph), Dodson did the same lap in 4 minutes 13 seconds (plus he had a 1 credit lap advantage). Manby-Colegrave moved ahead of Driscoll.

One of the first (of many) drivers to misjudge the corner where Queen's Parade turns into Main Street was H Weir in the Ford Special. He hit the sandbags but was able to lift the car back on the road and continue the race.

Goodacre (6) passes Weir (37) who hit the sandbags at the bottom of Main Street. Photo with thanks to the British Newspaper Archive.

The Charlie Goodacre Austin, the slowest of the three works cars, after only two laps retired with a broken throttle cable.

The Duke of Grafton was another early retirement. He stopped at the bottom of Main Street to try and fix the ailing engine of the Squire. He retired soon after, the engine having a burnt out valve.

Powys-Lybbe, Alfa Romeo, racing through Bangor.
Photo Bradley collection.

Powys-Lybbe was in front but not leading on handicap. After 20 minutes the positions on handicap were

1. Dodson, Austin (1 credit lap).

2. Sullivan, FIAT ((3 credit laps).

3. Powys-Lybbe, Alfa Romeo (zero credit laps).

4. ffrench Davis, FIAT (4 credit laps).

5. Driscoll, Austin (1 credit lap).

6. Fleming (MG) (5 credit laps).

There was a constant stream of cars going into the pits.

Manby-Colegrave in the ERA was a regular visitor to the pits trying to fix a misfire in the ERA engine. The problem returned but he kept going. However according to reports he failed to consistently produce the speed needed to threaten Powys-Lybbe.

Ivo Peters in the Frazer Nash was another frequent visitor to the pits with plug troubles but again was able to keep going. Driscoll in the second works Austin came in his 6th lap to get oil and went back out again.

By contrast L R Briggs in the MG, despite recurring plug/ignition trouble, stayed out of the pits. He was driving steadily, making no mistakes, and gradually moving up in position.

Powys-Lybbe continued to lap quickly and, with Dodson following close behind, was picking off the slower cars to move up the leader board. The two cars continued to battle it out. Dodson bettered the 1935 lap record by 5 seconds, his speed 84.51 mph. Powys-Lybbe's answer was to go even faster, first with a lap of 85.18 mph and later 86.56 mph. All the time Dodson was on his tail, averaging nearly 83 mph - 4 minutes 12 seconds ahead of his handicap.

On the 8th lap Driscoll stopped on the far side of the course. The second works Austin was out of the race with a broken oil pipe.

After 40 minutes Dodson remained in front on handicap but Powys-Lybbe had moved up into second place. Billy Sullivan (FIAT) had dropped down to third place. Hugh McFerran (Bugatti) and L R Briggs (MG) had moved up into 4th and 5th place respectively pushing ffrench Davis (FIAT) down into 6th position.

Disaster struck on Dodson's 11th lap when the last remaining works Austin retired with a broken piston. Well aware that his only serious challenger was gone Powys-Lybbe eased the pace (slightly) and continued to pass the slower cars he caught up with as he lapped.

McArthur (24) leads Baird (16) into Main Street.
Photo: UAC Archive.

Bobby Baird, (MG) had been going well up until he hit a dog at high speed damaging the steering. He continued going but was lapping slower than before and at around this time had to retire.

The corners at Clandeboye, Crawfordsburn and Queen's Parade going into Main Street were the source of much entertainment for spectators with many of the cars skidding and occasionally coming to grief.

Another popular spot was Bangor West railway bridge where if the car didn't go airborne you just were not trying hard enough. It was not easy to get a decent photograph of the cars in the air but some succeeded.

Given how newsworthy Arthur Conan Doyle and the Golden Bugatti were, it is not surprising that photographers got suitably dramatic action shots at both Bangor West and going into Main Street.

Conan Doyle and the Golden Bugatti airborne at Bangor West
and (below) skidding at Main Street.
Photos UAC Archive.

**A R Finlay (MG) correcting a skid at Clandeboye.
Photo UAC Archive.**

By the time the race had run for slightly over 50 minutes, seven cars had retired.

At the 60 minute mark Powys-Lybbe was in first place and, barring accidents or mechanical problems, could not be beaten. McFerran (Bugatti), driving for all he was worth, had worked his way up from fourth into second place. Briggs (MG), driving in his usual consistent and fast manner, moved up two places into third. Taylor (Bugatti) was in fourth, Conan Doyle (Bugatti) in fifth and Mangan (MG),was in sixth place.

McFerran's Bugatti's freshly rebuilt engine could not stick the pace and joined the ever increasing list of retirements. The list now also included Billy Sullivan (FIAT, burst radiator) and Trevor McCalla (Sullivan Special).

Malcom Fleming made one of his very few mistakes, spun the car and buckled a wheel. He made it back to the pits but by the time he rejoined the race he had moved down the leader board.

**Malcolm Fleming (32), MG, over does it at Clandeboye corner
and ends up facing the wrong way.
Photo author's collection.**

Jackie Chambers in the Riley had a difficult race and after several pit stops eventually retired. J Hutton Harrop, also in a Riley, retired (reason unknown). ffrench Davis called into the pits for a change of plugs and retired shortly afterwards.

By his 19th lap Powys-Lybbe was averaging 83.34 miles per hour and on the 20th lap passed the last remaining car in front of him on the road (Mangan).

36 seconds past 5 o'clock Anthony Powys-Lybbe in the 2,636 cc supercharged Alfa Romeo completed his 25th lap and took the chequered flag, winning the third County Down Trophy Race at an average speed of 84.36 mph.

His fastest lap was 86.56 mph, 3.69 mph faster than the previous record set in 1935 by Luis Fontés in the same car. Powys-Lybbe drove the entire race without calling into the pits, even to refuel.

A fraction over 4 minutes later, having completed 21 laps, L R Briggs crossed the finish line. Derrick Taylor in the Bugatti, who earlier had been desperately trying to get by Briggs, crossed the line (after 24 laps) 2 minutes and six seconds later.

Only 10 cars officially finished the race. The regulations allowed drivers 20 minutes to finish after the winner crossed the line.

Ivo Peters in the Frazer Nash completed his 22nd (and last) lap 11 seconds after the cutoff point. The UAC presented him with a finishers award anyway.

Opposite: Lord Craigavon, the Northern Ireland Prime Minister, places the laurel wreath on Anthony Powys-Lybbe.
Photo with thanks to the British Newspaper Archive.

L R Briggs came 2nd driving the Pellegrini Mille Miglia MG K3. Photo National Museums Northern Ireland.

When asked about his win, Anthony Powys-Lybbe said *"it was due to the old car knowing the course."*

The Alfa Romeo did not come out of the race unscathed. A crack was found in the chassis and had to be plated under the drivers seat. The price, no doubt, of going airborne at Bangor West railway bridge.

Wallace McLeod speculated on how the same car could be so much faster than it was in 1935 when driven by Luis Fontés. He ruled out any small changes to the course and thought it very unlikely that the car was significantly more highly tuned.

His conclusion was that the car had been better prepared and Anthony Powys-Lybbe was a much better driver.

The 1936 Results

	Name	Car	Time	MPH
1	A Powys-Lybbe	Alfa Romeo, 2,336 cc s/c	1 hr 45 min 36 secs	84.36
2	L R Briggs	MG, 1,087 cc s/c	1 hr 49 min 4 secs	75.15
3	D Taylor	Bugatti, 2,263 cc s/c	1 hr 51 min 10 secs	76.93
4	C H Manders	Adler, 995 cc	1 hr 51 min 43 secs	66.98
5	G A Mangan	MG, 847 cc	1 hr 52 min 4 secs	63.6
6	A P McArthur	MG, 1,287 cc	1 hr 54 min 4 secs	65.26
7	A Conan Doyle	Bugatti, 1,492 cc s/c	1 hr 55 min 3 secs	74.34
8	M Fleming	MG 847 cc	1 hr 55 min 26 secs	61.74
9	G F A Manby-Colegrave	ERA, 1488 cc s/c	2 hr 0 min 14 secs	74.10
10	J McGrattan	FIAT 995 cc	2 hr 2 min 47 secs	60.95

No team prize was awarded. Thirty-one cars started the race. The ten above were the official finishers. In addition Ivo Peters, Frazer Nash, completed his final lap 11 seconds too late to be counted as an official finisher.

Fifteen cars are mentioned in reports as retirements. According to Motor Sport (July 1936) there were nineteen retirements in total, which if there were thirty-one starters, leaves one car unaccounted for.

Drivers not listed as officially finishing

No	Name	Car	Reason
6	C Goodacre	Austin	Retired
7	C J P Dodson	Austin	Retired
8	L P Driscoll	Austin	Retired
10	C G Neill	Bugatti	?
11	Duke of Grafton	Squire	Retired
14	H C McFerran	Bugatti	Retired
15	A A Millard	ALTA	Retired
16	W R Baird	MG R Type	Retired
17	J R Morley	Bugatti	Retired
18	Ivo Peters	Frazer Nash	Outside time limit
19	J Chambers	Riley	Retired
20	J Hutton Harrup	Riley	Retired
21	W Sullivan	FIAT	Retired
22	A Hutchinson	MG PB	?
25	H W Furey	MG	?
26	A R Finlay	MG	?
27	F H ffrench Davis	FIAT	Retired
30	W T McCalla	Sullivan Special	Retired
35	T J McCall	MG	Retired
36	H B Prestwich	MG	?
37	H Weir	Ford	Retired

Best and last

That evening Caproni's in Bangor was packed. Viscountess Castlereagh distributed the prizes and was thanked on behalf of the competitors by Anthony Powys-Lybbe and Flight Lieutenant Briggs.

Viscount Castlereagh congratulated the club on achieving yet another big success. The Mayor of Bangor was equally vocal in his praise.

The Ulster Automobile Club was delighted. The race ran reasonably smoothly and, despite the very high speeds, there were no accidents resulting in serious injury, apart from one unfortunate dog. The number of spectators was even higher than the year before. All in all, there were grounds for celebration and the club was already planning the 1937 event.

Tragedy struck the Tourist Trophy race in September that year when a racing car crashed into spectators in Regent Street, Newtownards. Eight died and at least fifteen were seriously injured. There had been fatalities at motor races before but nothing as bad as this involving spectators. The future of road racing in Northern Ireland was now in doubt.

There would be no more TT races on the Ards course. In 1937 the RAC moved the race to Donington Park in England.

The loss of the TT races was a serious blow to Northern Ireland but it was not immediately clear what would happen to the County Down Trophy Race. The UAC response was to try and make the event even bigger and more important but they needed at the very least a road closing permit from Down County Council.

The County Down Trophy Race was viable because of the large numbers of spectators it attracted, many lining the streets of Bangor watching the racing cars pass just a few feet away, Clearly there was the risk of a car or cars going into group of spectators. A race course consisting purely of country roads would have less concentrated groups of spectators but, as most could watch for free, experience had shown that such events could not pay their way. The UAC waited for a decision from Down County Council.

In September 1936 a new roundabout was constructed at the junction of the Conlig/Belfast roads not far from the Down Trophy start line. Some thought it was deliberately done to make the existing road racing course unusable.

However the UAC knew at the beginning of the year that the roundabout was going to be built and felt it would have no significant impact on the race.

September 1936 saw a new roundabout at the end of Abbey Street not far from the start/finish line.
Photo UAC Archive.

In January 1937, 3 months after the roundabout was finished, the UAC were still hoping for a positive decision from Down County Council regarding the Bangor course. When it came Down County Council's decision was that no road closing orders would be granted for races in built up areas. This ended any hope of using the Bangor course again.

It did not end all motor sport in County Down or road racing in other County Council areas. The UAC continued to use Bangor as the finishing point for the Circuit of Ireland Trial (later Rally) for many years and existing hill climbs, for example Craigantlet, were not affected.

The UAC found a new course within the Antrim County Council area and, as it was no longer in County Down, gave the race a new name. In June 1937 the first International Ulster Trophy Race was held at Ballyclare, County Antrim. In 1946 the Ulster Trophy was the first international race held in the United Kingdom after World War 2.

The success of the Ulster Trophy Races at Ballyclare helped persuade the RAC to bring the TT races back to Northern Ireland in 1950 to a new road racing course at Dundrod. In 1953 the Ulster Grand Prix motorcycle race moved from Clady to Dundrod and Northern Ireland finally had the road racing course for both motorcycles and motor cars Harry Ferguson and others wanted in 1922.

Some of the cars that competed in the Down Trophy Races still exist including the three winners. The car that won the first County Down Trophy Race, the ex-Sir Henry Segrave Grand Prix Sunbeam, is on display in the Ulster Transport Museum at Cultra.

It is worth going to see and, when you do, imagine you are Trevor McCalla hurling the car around the Donaghadee course and winning that first County Down Trophy race.

Paul Robinson

November 2024

Bibliography

Title	Author	Publisher
Alfa Romeo Monza: The Autobiography of a Celebrated 8c-2300	Mick Walsh	Porter Press
The Ards Tourist Trophy Races	Bob Montgomery	Dreolín
Austin Racing History	Roland C Harrison	Motor Racing Publications Ltd
Bert Hadley A son of Birmingham	Compiled by Geoff Roe	The Pre-War Austin 7 Club
Brooklands to Goodwood	Rodney Waverley	Foulis
Bugatti Le pur-sang des automobiles	H G Conway	Foulis
The Bray Motor Races 1934-1935	Robin McCullagh	Dreolín
British Racing Green	David Venables	Ian Allan Publishing
The Complete Encyclopaedia of Motorcars	Edited by G N Georgano	Ebury Press
FIAT	Michael Sedgwick	Batsford
Green Dust	Brendan Lynch	Portobello
The Hawke History of MMM Competition Cars	Karl-Joachim Wiessmann	Directa Buldt

A History of Motorsport in Ireland	W A McMaster	Century Newspapers Ltd.
The History of Ulster Road Racing in focus	Eddie Mateer	Ulster Speed Promotions Ltd
The International Ulster Trophy Races 1934 - 1955	John S Moore	Dreolín
The Irish International Grand Prix 1929 - 31	Bob Montgomery	Dreoilín
A Racing Motorist	S C H Davis	Iliffe & Sons Ltd
Road versus Rail	P E Greer	Public Records Office Northern Ireland
The Story of ERA	John Lloyd	Motor Racing Publications Ltd
Sports Cars 1928 - 1939	T R Nicholson	Blanford Press London
Tourist Trophy	Richard Hough	Hutchinson of London
Tourist Trophy Replica Frazer Nash	John Teague	Profile Publications
Wheel Patter	Dudley Colley	Talbot Press, Dublin

Newspapers and magazines

Newspaper/magazine	Publication year
Autocar	1934 - 1936
Belfast News-Letter	1931-1937
Belfast Telegraph	1931-1937
Herald and Co Down Independent	1934-1936
Irish Auto Sport	1934
Light Car	1934 - 1936
UAC Monthly Review	1934-1937
The Motor News/Irish Motor News	1934-1936
Motor Sport	1934-1936
Newtownards Chronicle	1934-1936
The Newssheet UVCC	2018
Northern Whig	1931-1937
The Spectator	1934-1937

Websites

British Newspaper Archive	britishnewspaperarchive.co.uk
Motor Sport	motorsportmagazine.com
Lennonwylie	lennonwylie.co.uk
The story of the Vale Special	https://valespecial.net/
James Welsley Shaw	vintagenorton.com

Appendix 1

Index of entrants & drivers 1934 to 1936

D: Driver
E: Entrant only
ED: Entrant and driver
R: Reserve driver
DNR: Did not race
DNQ: Did not qualify

Name			Car	Year
G Abecassis	D	England	Austin 747 cc s/c	1935 DNR
Almack Engineering	E	London	Austin 747 cc s/c	1935 DNR
	E		Riley 1,089 cc	1936
J P Almack	D	England	Riley 1,089 cc	1936 DNQ
W F Ayrton	ED	Belfast	MG 1250 cc	1934
	ED		MG 1,287 cc	1935
Sir Herbert Austin	E	B'ham	Austin 747 cc s/c	1935
	E		Austin 744 cc s/c	1936
	E		Austin 744 cc s/c	1936
	E		Austin	1936
W R (Bobby) Baird	ED	Belfast	Riley 1,087 cc	1934
	ED		MG 747 cc s/c	1935
	ED		MG R type 750 cc	1936
W D Banks	ED	N'ards	Bentley	1934
J C Bartlett	R	Northern Ireland	C & T Special 1,497 cc	1935

P Bartlett	E	Northern Ireland	C & T Special 1,497 cc	1935
W A Bartlett	D	Northern Ireland	C & T Special 1,497 cc	1935
J Bell	D	Northern Ireland	C&T Special s/c	1936 DNQ
L R Briggs	ED ED ED	Green-island	MG 847 cc MG 847 cc MG 1,087 cc s/c	1934 1935 1936
Archibald Carr	ED	Belfast	Lagonda de Clifford Special 1,084 cc	1935
F Cassidy	D		MG 847 cc	1936 DNQ
Jack Chambers	ED ED	Belfast	Riley 1,089 cc Riley 1,089 cc	1935 1936
R Cavanagh	R	Dublin	Ford 993 cc	1936 DNR
Adrian Conan Doyle	D	England	Bugatti 1,492 cc s/c	1936
Denis Conan Doyle	R	England	Bugatti 1,492 cc s/c	1936
S C Collier	ED	New York	MG Magnette 1,087 cc s/c	1935
Ian F Connell	ED	London	Vale 1,496 cc s/c	1935
Alan Corry	D	see Lloyd Cowdy	MG Magna	1934
Lloyd Cowdy	D	Entered as Alan Corry	MG Magna	1934

214

Dick & Co	E	Belfast	FIAT	1935
Austin Dobson	ED	London	Alfa Romeo 2,336 cc s/c	1935
C J P Dodson	D	England	Austin 744 cc	1936
P Donnelly	D	Dublin	Riley 1,089 cc	1934
L P Driscoll	D	London	Austin 747 cc s/c	1935
	D		Austin 744 cc s/c	1936
Philip Dwyer	ED	Cahir, Ireland	Bugatti, 3,255 cc	1935
F W Earney	ED	N'ards	Amilcar	1934
A R Finlay	ED	Bangor	MG Magna 1,087 cc	1934
	ED		MG Magna 1,087 cc	1936
F ffrench Davis	D	Dublin	FIAT 995 cc	1935
	ED		FIAT 995 cc	1936
Luis Fontés	ED	London	Alfa Romeo 2,336 cc s/c	1935
M (Malcolm) H Fleming	ED	Belfast	MG 847 cc	1934
	ED		MG 847 cc	1935
	ED		MG 847 cc	1936
J Furey	E	Bangor	MG Magnette 1,287 cc	1935
H W (Walter) Furey	D	Bangor	MG Magnette 1,287 cc	1935
	ED		MG Magnette 1,287 cc	1936
J E Gibson	R	Dublin	Ford 3,622 cc	1935

Charles Goodacre	R D	England	Austin 747 cc s/c	1935
			Austin 744 cc s/c	1936
N F Gordon	R	?	MG 1250 cc	1934
Duke of Grafton	ED	London	Squire 1496 cc s/c	1936
D C Gracey	E	Lurgan	C & T Special 1,497 cc	1936
E Griffiths-Hughes	ED	London	Frazer Nash 1,496 cc	1935
J Hulton Harrop	R	London	Riley 1,089 cc	1936
John R Hodge	ED ED	London	Singer 972 cc MG Magnette 1,287 cc	1934 1935
Alan Hutchinson	D	Northern Ireland	MG PB 939 cc s/c	1936
K N Hutchinson	ED	England	Ford 3,622 cc	1935
L Innis	ED	Holywood, Co Down	Morris Minor	1934
Irischer Alder Renstall	E	Ireland	Alder 995 cc	1936
W J Kavanagh	ED	Dublin	Riley 1,089 cc	1934
L Liddel	E	Belfast	MG 847 cc	1936 DNR
AP McArthur	ED	Sligo	MG Magnette 1,287 cc	1936
D Mackenzie	ED	Dublin	Riley 1,089 cc	1934
D C MacLachlan	ED	Cork	Riley 1,089 cc	1934
G F A Manby -Colegrave	ED	London	MG 1,087 cc	1935 DNR
	ED		ERA 1488 cc s/c	1936

Charles Manders	D	Ireland	Adler 995 cc	1936
G A Mangan	D	Ireland	MG P Type 847 cc	1936
Princess Nina Mdivani	E	Crowborough	Bugatti 1,492 cc s/c	1936
A A Millard	ED	Cambridge	ALTA 1,074 cc s/c	1936
W M D Montgomery	E	Ballymena	Wolseley Hornet	1934
Mervyn White Services	E		Bugatti 2,270 cc s/c	1936
J R Morley	ED	Weybridge	Bugatti 1,496 cc	1936
J McArdle	ED	Belfast	MG	1934
T J McCall	ED	Holywood, Co Down	MG P Type 847 cc	1936
W T (Trevor) McCalla	ED	Crossgar	Sunbeam 1,998 cc s/c	1934
	ED		Sunbeam 1,998 cc s/c	1935
	D		Sullivan Special 849 cc s/c	1936
H (Hugh) C McFerran	ED	Belfast	Bugatti 1,990 cc	1934
	E		MG Magna	1934
	ED		Bugatti 1,990 cc	1935
	ED		Bugatti 1,990 cc	1936
J McGrattan	ED	Bangor	MG 847 cc	1934
	ED		MG 847 cc	1935
	ED		FIAT 995 cc	1936
C G Neill	ED	Belfast	Bugatti 1,900 cc	1934 DNR
	ED		Bugatti 1,990 cc	1935
	ED		Bugatti 1,990 cc	1936

T O'Shaughnessy	E	Dublin	Riley	1934
R E Parish	R	Belfast	Wolseley Hornet 1,271 cc	1935
J W Patterson	ED	Belfast	Wolseley Hornet 1,271 cc	1934 DNR
	E		MG PB 939 cc s/c	1936
Ivo Peters	ED	Bristol	Frazer Nash 1,496 cc	1936
Anthony Powys -Lybbe	ED	Bradfield	Alfa Romeo 2,336 cc s/c	1936
H B Prestwich	ED	Altringham	MG J3 847 cc	1936
C Quigley	D	Ireland	Ford 993 cc	1936
G Rand	R	USA	MG Magnette 1,087 cc s/c	1935
N G Robinson	ED	Belfast	Wolseley Hornet 1,271 cc	1935 DNR
E Robb	D	Ulster	MG Magnette 1,287 cc	1936
Robin A Scott	ED	Belfast	MG 847 cc	1935
J Welsley Shaw	ED	Belfast	Triumph 1,271 s/c	1935
S R Sheane	ED	Wicklow	MG P Type 847 cc	1936
Smithfield Motor Co Ltd	E	Dublin	Ford 993 cc	1936
F Smyth	ED	Belfast	Ford 993 cc	1935 DNR
	E		Ford 993 cc	1936

W (Billy) Sullivan	ED	Belfast	Sullivan Special 739 cc S/C	1934
	D		Bugatti 1,990 cc	1935
	ED		FIAT 995 cc	1936
	E		Sullivan Special 849 cc s/c	1936
Derrick Taylor	ED	London	Bugatti 1,496 cc	1935
	ED		Bugatti 2,263 cc	1936
J Tookey	D	Dublin	Ford 993 cc	1936 DNR
H Weir	D	Northern Ireland	Ford 993 cc	1936
Mervyn White	D	Chalfont St Peter	Bugatti 2,270 cc s/c	1936
P N Whitehead	ED	Cambridge	ERA 1.488 cc s/c	1936
A H Wilkinson	E	Belfast	Singer 972 cc	1934
E Wilkinson	D	Belfast	Singer 972 cc	1934
W H Wilson	R	Belfast	Bugatti 1,900 cc	1935
David Yule	ED	Dublin	Austin 747 cc s/c	1934 DNR

Appendix 2

OFFICIALS for each year

County Down Trophy 30 June 1934

Colonel F Lindsay LLoyd, CMG, DSO - RAC	RAC Steward
P S Brady - President IMRC	Steward
F H Rogers - Chairman Ulster TT Committee	Steward
Wm Noble - Chairman UAC	Steward
W J Chambers	Judge
R McCann	Judge
R McCondell	Judge
Captain W J Thompson	Clerk of course and secretary of the meeting
J M Thompson	Chief marshal
H A Byrson,	Chief flag marshal
W W McLeod AMIAE	Chief depot manager and official scruntineer
W P E Alexander	Depot marshal
E A Swinson	Depot marshal
C G Pinkerton	Depot marshal
C A Stewart	Depot marshal
Dr H F Northey	Chief Medical Officer

Dr Johnstone	Medical Officer
Dr Moore	Medical Officer
Dr McMechan	Medical Officer
Dr Boyd	Medical Officer
Dr McKeown	Medical Officer
Dr Page	Medical Officer
Dr Campbell	Medical Officer
Dr Liggett	Medical Officer
Dr Hannah	Medical Officer
Dr O'Kane	Medical Officer
Dr Armstrong	Medical Officer
J Robertson	Chief enclosure marshal
R H Wright	Chief timekeeper
A H Wilkinson	Travelling marshal
E M Kilpatrick	Press steward
Captain R A H Tougher	Press steward
Captain R L Henderson	Public announcer
M J McCoull	Control officer
F McDowell	Assistant control officer
J McMurray	Assistant control officer
W J White	Zone marshal - McCoubrey's corner

S Q Osborne	Zone marshal - Angus corner
T Stewart	Zone marshal - Donaghadee hairpin
G Shields	Programme steward
D Mcferran	Programme steward
C G Neill	Clerk of the scoreboard
C W R McCreary	Scoreboard assistant
B L Wylie	Scoreboard assistant
F Ward	Scoreboard assistant

International County Down Trophy Race 22 June 1935

OFFICIALS (as listed in the official programme)

Stewards of the Meeting

Rt Hon J Milne Barbour DL MP

Walter Malcolm (Mayor of Bangor)

Capt. A W Phillips MC

F H Rogers

Judges

W J Chambers

R Condell

Chief Marshal

W Noble

Chief Flag Marshal

H A Byrson

Chief Depot Marshal and Official Scrutineer

W W McLeod AMIAE

Depot Marshals

W P E Alexander

T E Burke-Murphy

C G Pinkerton

C A Stuart

Chief Medical Officer

H F Northey MB, BCh.

Medical Officers

C J A Woodside, MB, MCh, FRCS

H P Malcolm, MB, MCh, FRCS

Dr G Gray

Dr F Kane

Dr R Moore

Dr F Turner

Dr W Loughridge

Dr A Moore

Dr E McMeekin

Dr W Hanna

Dr J F Johnstone

Dr J Darling

Dr T K Armstrong

Dr J M O'Kane

Dr B Boal

Dr H R D Ireland

Dr W Page

Dr W Campbell

Dr H H Collier

Dr J F McKeown

Chief Enclosure Marshal

J Robertson

Chief Timekeeper

R H Wright

Assistant Timekeepers

W Gunning

H Oliver ACA

T Walker Jackson

Miss E McGowan

W McD Taylor

Miss E I Wright

G F Hall

Press Steward

R McCann, JP

Public Announcer

Capt R L Henderson

Control Officer

J McMurray

Assistant Control Officers

W J McCracken

F N McDowell

W H McGiffin

Zone Marshals

T Stewart (Clandeboye)

S Q Osbourne (Crawfordstown)

C Duffin (Bangor West)

Zone Marshals continued

W J White (Queen's Parade)

Programme Steward

G Shields

Clerks of the Scoreboard

H W Taggart

R D White

J C Conway

Clerk of the Course and Secretary of the Meeting

Capt W J Thompson

International County Down Trophy Race 20 June 1936

Officials - as published in the UAC Monthly Review June 1936

Stewards of the meeting

Viscount Castlereagh DL MP

The Right Hon J Milne Barbour DL MP

Captain A W Philips MC

Walter Malcolm Esq

F H Rogers Esq

Judge

Mr R Condell

Chief Marshal

Alderman W J Chambers

Chief depot Marshall and Official Scrutineer

W W McLeod AMIAE

Chief Medical Officer

Dr Northey

Timekeeping

Mr R H Wright and his capable staff

Control Officer

Mr W J White

Travelling Marshal

Mr A H Wilkinson

Director of Establishments

Mr W Noble

Clerk of the Course and Secretary of the Meeting

Captain W J Thompson

Driver lists 1934 to 1936

1934 County Down Trophy Race driver list - 23 entered

Based on Belfast News-Letter 19 June 1934

1	W T McCalla	Crossgar	Sunbeam s/c
2	H C McFerran	Belfast	Bugatti
3	W R Baird	Belfast	Riley
4	D C MacLachlan	Cork	Riley
5	W J Kavanagh	Dublin	Riley
6	D Mackenzie	Dublin	Riley
7	P Donnelly	Dublin	Riley
8	A Corry	Belfast	MG Magna
9	W Sulivan	Belfast	Sullivan Special s/c
11	A R Finlay	Bangor	MG Magna
12	David Yule	Dublin	Austin s/c
14	E J Wilkinson	Belfast	Singer
15	J R Hodge	London	Singer
16	W F Ayrton	Belfast	MG
17	Flight Lieut. L R Briggs	Belfast	MG
18	J McGrattan	Bangor	MG

19	M H Fleming	Belfast	MG
21	F W Earney	Newtownards	Amilcar
	W D Banks	Newtownards	Bentley
	L Innis	Holywood	Morris minor
	A R Kennedy	England	MG s/c
	J McArdle	Belfast	MG
	J W Patterson	Ballymena	Wolseley Hornet

Notes

There were 23 entries. The maximum number of entrants permitted by the RAC was 20.

A R Kennedy and W D Banks are not listed as taking part in the practice on 28th June - I assume they withdrew their entries before practice which brings the number of drivers down to 21.

The Light Car (29 June 1934 page 186) lists 2 reserve entrants - J McArdle and L Innis. Both did not turn for practice and therefore did not qualify. In addition two drivers, D Yule and J W Patterson crashed during practice and failed to qualify.

The 17 remaining drivers took part in the race.

The Ulster Automobile Club did not use the number 13 when allocating race numbers.

1935 International County Down Trophy Race - Full entry list (as per official programme)

No: Race number
D: Driver
E: Entrant only
ED: Entrant and driver
R: Reserve driver

No	Name		Car	Engine cc	H'cap Laps
1	Luis Fontés	ED	Alfa Romeo s/c	2,336	0
2	Austin Dobson	ED	Alfa Romeo s/c	2,600	0
3	G F A Manby-Colegrave	ED	MG Magnette s/c	1,087	1
4	W T McCalla	ED	Sunbeam s/c	1,992	1
5	I F Connell	ED	Vale s/c	1,496	1
6	S C Collier G Rand	ED R	MG Magnette s/c	1,087	1
7	H C McFerran W H Wilson	ED R	Bugatti	1,990	1
8	W R Baird	ED	MG Midget s/c	750	2
9	Sir H Austin L P Driscoll C L Goodacre	E D R	Austin s/c	747.5	2
10	P Dwyer	ED	Bugatti	3,255	2
11	C G Neill	ED	Bugatti	1,990	2

12	H C McFerran W Sullivan	E D	Bugatti	1,990	2
14	Capt D Taylor	ED	Bugatti	1,496	2
15	E Griffiths Hughes	ED	Frazer Nash	1,496	3
16	K N Hutchinson J E Gibson	ED R	Ford	3,622	3
17	J Chambers	ED	Riley	1,089	3
18	J Wesley Shaw	ED	Triumph s/c	1,232	3
19	W F Ayrton	ED	MG Magnette	1,287	4
20	Almack Engineering Services G Abecassis P Almack	E D R	Austin s/c	747	4
21	Conquor & Topping W A Bartlett J C Bartlett	E D R	C&T Special	1,497	4
22	H W Furey	ED	MG Magnette	1,287	4
23	J R Hodge	ED	MG Magnette	1,287	4
24	Archibald Carr	ED	Lagonda	1,084	4
25	L R Briggs	ED	MG Midget	847	5
26	Dick & Co F H ffrench Davis J F Sutherland	E D R	FIAT	995	5
27	N G Robinson R E Parish	ED R	Wolseley	1,271	5

28	R A Scott	ED	MG	847	6
29	M H Fleming	ED	MG	847	6
30	J McGrattan	ED	MG	847	6
31	F Smyth	ED	Ford	993	6

Note: The Ulster Automobile Club did not use the number 13 when allocating race numbers.

MG Magnette engine capacity clarification

I am grateful to Simon Johnston for the following:

With the new N Type Magnette, launched in 1934, M.G. introduced a new six-cylinder engine of 1,287cc. However, all was not what it seemed as the engine was actually 1,271cc, not 1,287cc. M.G. were concerned lest prospective buyers might think the new engine was the same as the generally inferior 1,271cc engine that was fitted to contemporary Wolseleys. They therefore simply increased the declared stroke of the engine from 83mm to 84mm in order to increase the capacity to a notional 1,287cc. This fiction even extended to the NE Magnettes entered in the 1934 and 1935 TTs, all of which had a declared capacity of 1,287cc.

I have used the declared engine capacity of 1,287 cc throughout this book.

1936 Entry list including drivers. As published in the UAC Monthly Review June 1936.

D: Driver
E: Entrant only
ED: Entrant and driver
R: Reserve driver

Name	E D R	Car	Engine cc
Almack Engineering Ltd	E	Riley	1,089
J P Almack	D	Riley	1,089
Sir Herbert Austin	E	Austin s/c	744
Sir Herbert Austin	E	Austin s/c	744
Sir Herbert Austin	E	Austin s/c	744
J Bell	D	C&T Special	1,497
J P Driscoll	D	Austin s/c	744
C L Goodacre	D	Austin s/c	744
C J P Dodson	D	Austin s/c	744
W R Baird	ED	MG R Type	750
L R Briggs	ED	MG s/c	1,087
F Cassidy	D	MG	847
Adrian Conan Doyle	D	Bugatti s/c	1492
J Chambers	ED	Riley	1,089

G F A Manby-Colegrave	ED	ERA s/c	1,488
F H ffrench Davis	ED	FIAT	995
A R Finlay	ED	MG	1,087
M H Fleming	ED	MG	847
H W Furey	ED	MG	1,087
D C Gracey	E	C&T Special	1,497
Duke of Grafton	ED	Squire s/c	1496
Irischer Alder Renstall	E	Adler	995
L Liddel	E	MG	847
A Powys-Lybbe	ED	Alfa Romeo s/c	2,336
Charles Manders	D	Adler	995
Princess Nina Mdivani	E	Bugatti s/c	1492
A P McArthur	ED	MG Magnette	1,287
G A Mangan	D	MG P Type	847 cc
A A Millard	ED	ALTA	1,087
T J McCall	ED	MG P Type	847
W T McCalla	D	Sullivan Special s/c	849
H C McFerran	ED	Bugatti	1990
J McGrattan	ED	FIAT	995
J R Morley	ED	Bugatti	1,496
C G Neill	ED	Bugatti	1,990
J W Patterson	ER	MG PB s/c	939

Ivo Peters	ED	Frazer Nash	1,496
H B Prestwich	ED	MG J3	847
S R Sheane	E	MG P Type	847
Smithfield Motor Co Ltd.	E	Ford	993
F Smyth	E	Ford	993
W Sullivan	ED E	FIAT Sullivan Special s/c	995 849
H Weir	D	Ford	993
D Taylor	ED	Bugatti s/c	2,263
Mervyn White Services	E	Bugatti s/c	2,270
Mervyn White	D	Bugatti s/c	2,270
PN Whitehead	ED	ERA s/c	1,488

Notes :

J P Almack (Riley) did not qualify and reserve driver Hutton-Harrup was the driver in the race itself.

J Patterson. MG PB, also did not qualify as a reserve driver and the name of the "young Ulsterman" entered to drive it was withheld on the entry form. I think it was A Hutchinson.

One other reserve driver, J W Shiel, failed to qualify. I don't know who he was the reserve driver for.

1936 International County Down Trophy Race Drivers

This is the list of the thirty one drivers who I believe competed on 20 June 1936. Race numbers have been identified using photographs.

No	Name	Car
1	A Powys-Lybbe	Alfa Romeo s/c
3	G F A Manby-Colegrave	ERA s/c
5	D Taylor	Bugatti s/c
6	Charles Goodacre	Austin s/c
7	C J P Dodson	Austin s/c
8	Pat Driscoll	Austin s/c
9	Adrian Conan Doyle	Bugatti s/c
10	C G Neill	Bugatti
11	Duke of Grafton	Squire s/c
12	L R Briggs	MG s/c
14	H C McFerran	Bugatti
15	A A Millard	ALTA
16	W R Baird	MG R Type
17	J R Morley	Bugatti
18	Ivo Peters	Frazer Nash
19	J Chambers	Riley
20	J Hutton Harrop	Riley
21	W Sullivan	FIAT

22	A Hutchinson	MG PB s/c
24	A P McArthur	MG Magnette
25	H W Furey	MG
26	A R Finlay	MG
27	F H ffrench Davis	FIAT
28	Charles Manders	Adler
30	W T McCalla	Sullivan Special s/c
31	J McGrattan	FIAT
32	M H Fleming	MG
33	G A Mangan	MG P Type
35	T J McCall	MG P Type
36	H B Prestwich	MG J3
37	H Weir	Ford

Note: The Ulster Automobile Club did not use the number 13 when allocating race numbers.

Bangor Motor Sports Committee

Chairman:

THE MAYOR OF BANGOR (COUNCILLOR WALTER MALCOLM)

Joint Secretaries:

R M Moore, Esq., T B Graham, Esq

Hon. Tresurer and Organiser:

H Rogers, Esq

Members:

Alderman T Bailie	J Greer, Esq
Alderman R M Bowman	T Mann, Esq
Alderman W J Bradley	R Miley, Esq
Alderman J Cathy	J S Millar, Esq
Councillor S S Handforth	F Morgan, Esq
Councillor F Logan	G Morris , Esq
J T D Boyd, Esq	F G Ward, Esq
H L Caproni, Esq	T C G Richardson, Esq
D W Ewing, Esq	W Weir, Esq
S H Forrest, Esq	W J White, Esq
W Furey, Esq	W Watt, Esq

Back cover: The Vale Special , Abbey Street, Bangor 1935.
Photo Johnson collection.